医学部編入への英語演習

河合塾 KALS 監修／土田 治 著

講談社

序　文

　筆者が，河合塾KALSの医学部学士編入講座の英語を担当することになってから，もう10年くらいが経過したと思われます．毎年，主要大学の入試問題の解答を作成し，受講生の方にその解説をさせて頂きました．一方で，この仕事を続けていくうちに，いろいろな事情で講座を受講できないが，どうしても学士試験を目指したいという方が数多くいらっしゃるということを知りました．受講生だけでなく，こうした方々にも，学士試験の過去問を紹介し，少しでも力になれないかという思いが年々強くなっていきました．

　そうした時に，河合塾KALSの医学部学士編入講座で生命科学を担当されている井出冬章先生のお力添えで，講談社サイエンティフィクの三浦様より，この問題集のお話を頂きました．このようなお話を頂けたのも，井出先生が2008年に執筆された「医学部編入への生命科学演習」(講談社)が，いまだに多くの受験生から支持されているおかげだと思っております．

　本書で紹介されている問題は，転載許可が下りた実際の学士試験の過去問であり（問題5のみ学士試験ではなく，大学院入試です），解答が付いています．転載を快諾して頂いた大学関係者の方々にはこの場を借りて厚く御礼申し上げます．解答は，河合塾KALSの講座用にこれまで作成してきたものに手を加えて作成したものです．過去問を解き，答え合わせをするという作業は，受験勉強において必須の要素であり，ぜひ本書を有効に活用して頂きたいと思います．巻末には学士試験で覚えて頂きたい重要単語リストを載せていますので，そちらも役立てて頂きたいと思います．なお，各設問で取り上げている学術英語論文に関しましては，権利の関係上，全訳を載せることができませんでした．その分，解答・解説を詳しくしましたので，読者の皆様にはご了承頂きたいと思います．

　本書の執筆に当たっては，多くの方々のお世話になりました．前述の通り，本書は井出先生のご尽力がなければ，世に出ることはなかったと思っております．同じく医学部学士編入講座の永川隆史先生からの有益なアドバイスなしには，本書の執筆はできなかったと思います．また，KALSの事務局の方々にも大変お世話になりました．いつも過去問やそれに関連する情報や資料をきちんとまとめて下さり，解答作成をしやすい環境を作って頂きました．また，過去問を提供してくださった受講生にも深く感謝しております．さらに，解答作成の際には受講生の質問や意見から重大なヒントを頂いたこともよくありました．歴代の受講生の方には改めて御礼申し上げます．

　最後になりましたが，講談社サイエンティフィクの三浦様には，大変お世話になりました．筆者の執筆が遅れがちになり，多大なご迷惑やご心配をおかけしたにも関わらず，絶えず有益なアドバイスをして頂きました．厚く御礼申し上げます．

2013年3月

　　　　　　　　　　　　　　　　　　　　　　　　　　　　　　　　　　　土田　治

医学部編入への英語演習　目次

序文 iii

医学部学士試験の英語の特徴と勉強法 vi

第1章　設問形式別問題演習 1

1.1　和訳問題・内容説明問題 1

【問題1】《肥満に関する遺伝学》　愛媛大学　平成14年 1
【問題2】《放射線とがんの関係》　愛媛大学　平成16年 3
【問題3】《CTスキャンとがんの関係》　鹿児島大学　平成23年 5
【問題4】《神経の働きと記憶》　新潟大学　平成19年 10

1.2　要約問題 13

【問題5】《微生物とメタゲノミクス》　東京工業大学大学院　平成20年 13
【問題6】《遺伝子検査》　鹿児島大学　平成20年 15

1.3　選択式問題 18

【問題7】《病院衛生》　高知大学　平成17年 18

1.4　英作文 22

【問題8】《医学生と医師の関係》　旭川医科大学　平成17年 22
【問題9】《科学とは》　浜松医科大学　平成15年 28
【問題10】《医科学一般》　島根大学　平成22年 29

第2章 テーマ別問題演習 30

2.1 医師と患者の関係 30
【問題11】《医師と患者のコミュニケーション》　新潟大学　平成21年 30
【問題12】《HeLa細胞と研究倫理》　東海大学医学部一般編入試験　平成23年 33

2.2 最新医療技術 37
【問題13】《ヒトゲノム解読とオーダーメイド医療》　千葉大学　平成19年 37
【問題14】《ES細胞とiPS細胞》　千葉大学　平成23年 42

2.3 現代において問題となっている疾患 47
【問題15】《遺伝性疾患》　愛媛大学　平成21年 47
【問題16】《糖尿病》　愛媛大学　平成23年 49
【問題17】《環境と疾病の関係》　新潟大学　平成21年 52
【問題18】《アルツハイマー病》　高知大学　平成21年 55
【問題19】《感染症》　鹿児島大学　平成15年 62

解答・解説 65

重要単語リスト 147
§1　テーマ別重要単語リスト 147
§2　学士試験合格のために覚えておきたい重要単語 171
§3　知っておくと参考になる接頭辞と接尾辞 181

索引 183

医学部学士試験の英語の特徴と勉強法

1 医学部学士編入試験の英語の特徴
大学入試と比べてみると，次のような特徴が挙げられる．
(1) 単語が難しい．
(2) 細かな文法的知識は不要．
(3) 問題量に対する制限時間が短い．
(4) 出題される英文のテーマは，医学や生命科学に関するものが大半を占める．
(5) 記述式の問題（和訳，内容説明，要約など）が中心である．英作文が出る大学は少数．

2 医学部学士編入試験で必要な5つの力

(1) 単語力	(2) 文法力	(3) 予備知識力	(4) 読解力・速読力	(5) 記述力（答案作成能力）

(1) 単語力
まずは大学受験レベルの基本英単語を復習・暗記することがポイントになる．学士試験では，医療系，生命科学系の英文が出題されることが多いので，これらの専門単語を覚える必要もある．本書の単語リストを利用してほしい．専門単語ばかり覚えて，大学入試レベルの基本単語が疎かになるという逆転現象は避けたい．

〔補足〕単語の覚え方
単語帳を使う人もいれば，文章を読みながら覚える人もいる．また，CD等を使って耳から覚える人もいる．自分に合った方法を見つけること．どの方法をとるにせよ，速くくり返すことが大切である．なお，読解問題を解いた際に，わからない単語を書き出して後で復習できるようにしておくことも大切である．

(2) 文法力
正確な和訳力を身につけるために，高校で習う英文法を復習しておく．まずは，基本5文型，受動態，不定詞，動名詞，分詞，関係代名詞，無生物主語構文を復習しておけばよいだろう．なお，純粋な文法問題を出題する大学はほとんどない．ただし，滋賀医科大学はiBT以前のTOEFLで出題されていたような文法問題を出題する．

(3) 予備知識力
学士試験では，出題された英文のテーマに関する予備知識がないと苦しい場合が多い．普段から医療や生命科学に関する話題をチェックし，予備知識を蓄積していく必要がある．もっとも，学士試験を目指す人は生命科学の勉強をたっぷり行うことになるので，必然的に知識力は上がっていき，英語にも生かされることになる．

〔補足〕学士試験でよく利用される科学雑誌（Nature, Scienceなど）や医学雑誌（NEJMやLancet）に目を通すべきか．
⇒目を通せることが理想である．重要な話題をチェックでき，予備知識や単語も増える．

ただし，英語が得意でない人は，記事の題名に使われている単語をチェックするとか，Nature Digest で話題をチェックするくらいに留めてよい．

(4) 読解力・速読力

　医療系，生命科学系の英文をたくさん読み，慣れていく必要がある．医学部学士試験の英語は大学入試に比べて制限時間が短い．よって速読力が重要となる．次のことに注意してほしい．

　①単語力や予備知識力を充実させる．

　　　知っている単語ばかりの英文や，知っているテーマに関する英文は速く読める．

　②1文1文の文構造を捉えるスピードを上げていく．

　　　市販されている速読関連の本には，段落の最初と最後だけを読めばその段落の内容がわかると書かれていることがある．しかし，このような飛ばし読みの発想は，学士試験の英語では通用しづらい．まずは，1文1文を読み取るスピードを着実に速くしていくという地道な態度で勉強してほしい．

　③できるだけ戻り読みを避け，語順通りに意味を捉えていく（頭の中できれいな日本語に直しながら読んではいけない）．

　　　音読をすると，戻れないので，よい訓練になる．医療系のニュースを英語で聞き取るという訓練もよいかもしれない．

　④わかりづらい箇所が出てきた時に，そこで止まらずに，次の文や次の段落に進む．

　　　読み進めることで，後から意味がわかってくる場合がたくさんある．少し考えてわかりづらい場合には，先へ進み，時間をロスしないようにしたい．

　⑤問題文の表題や設問，語注，出典を先に見る．

　　　こうすることで，英文の内容を最初にある程度まで予測することができ，読みやすくなるであろう．これは，問題を解く際の基本なのでしっかり行ってほしい．

(5) 記述力（答案作成能力）

　学士試験の英語は，英文を和訳する力や，和訳した英文を問題の要求に応じて編集する力がないと対応できない．英文を理解できることと，答案を書けることはイコールにはならないので注意が必要．センター試験やTOEIC・TOEFLの読解問題で高得点を取っている人でも油断はできない．本書に出ている学士試験の過去問などを実際に解いて答案作りの練習をする必要がある．

3　英語に抵抗がない人へ

　学士試験を受験する人の中には，英語に抵抗がない人もたくさんいるであろう．こうした方々は，学士試験の過去問をやったり，（受験可能ならば）KALSの模試を受けたりして，2で説明した5つの力がそろっているかをさらっと確認してほしい．普通，上記のような人々は (1) の大学入試レベルの単語力や (2) (4) の力はすでに十分なので，医療系の単語力や (3) (5) を中心的に鍛え上げるということになる．英語に抵抗がない人でも，医療系の英単語や予備知識に精通しているとは限らないし，記述力が優れているとも限らない．自分が鍛え上げるべきポイントをしっかりと見極めてほしい．

　なお，帰国子女の人の中には，特に (5) の力を磨くことに苦労する人がいる．たとえば，知っ

ている単語なのに，日本語で表現できないという人がよくいる．こういう人は，大学受験用の単語帳を利用して，各英単語の日本語訳を1つ1つ確認する必要がある．また，大学受験用の和訳問題集の解答例をたくさん見て，和訳のパターンを覚えていく必要がある．

4　英語に抵抗がある人へ

英語に抵抗がある人とは，だいたい2の（1）（2）が不十分な人だと思ってもらいたい．こういう人は，まずは平均点を少し上回るくらいの点数（皆ができそうな簡単な問題は確実に解ける）を目指して頑張ってほしい．英語がこれくらいできれば，後は理科の頑張り次第でどうにでもなる．そのためには，次のような対策を地道に行っていく必要がある．

（1）大学受験用の有名な単語帳に出ている単語を9割以上覚える．

これをやらないとスムーズに英語は読めないし，文法や和訳の勉強をしようにも，わからない単語がたくさん出てきて嫌になる．最初のうちは，単語の勉強に毎日，十分な時間をかけたほうがよい．

・参考図書『ターゲット1900』旺文社

（2）（1）の作業をメインにしつつ，短文を和訳するという作業を行う．

英語に抵抗がある人は，いきなり長い文を読むのは大変であろうから，短文を訳す作業を行うことからはじめればよい．文法の重要論点が含まれている短文を和訳し，文法の基礎も復習する．慣れてきたら徐々に長い英文にも取り組んでいく．

（3）大学入試で出題された医療系の長文問題を解く

解き終わったら，わからない単語のチェックをする．また，全文の意味がわかるかを，文法に注意しながらチェックする（余裕があれば全訳を作ってみる）．その後は，すぐに各文の構造や訳が頭に浮かぶようになるくらいまで音読をくり返す（意味がわかった英文をくり返し読むことは極めて重要）．こうした感じで，長文問題を10〜20題くらい解けば英語力は確実につくであろう．要は，完璧にわかる英文を10〜20個作ってほしいということである．そして，それらの中で出てきた単語や文法事項が試験に出れば，確実に対応できるという状態を作ってほしい．

・参考図書
『医学部受験の読解演習』河合出版，渡辺英生・Rhodric Davies 著
『医歯薬系英単語　入試によくでる600』中経出版，船岡富有子著
『合格する！医歯薬への英語』東京コア，西村真澄著

|4のまとめ|：（1）は全員に必要な作業である．（2）（3）に関しては個人差が出るだろう．おそらく（2）を経ないでいきなり（3）の作業に入る人もいるであろう．（3）の作業をできるだけ早く終えて，学士試験の過去問に取り組めるようになるとよい．

5　最後に

学士試験では，生命科学の勉強にかなりの時間を割かねばならない．よって，英語の勉強に十分時間を取れない場合が出てくる．しかし，必ず，毎日，1分でもよいので英語に触れてほしい．毎日続けることが，英語の場合は大切である．

第1章
設問形式別問題演習

1.1 和訳問題・内容説明問題

【問題 1】 以下の英文を読んで問に答えなさい．
愛媛大学　平成14年　378語　30分

　　The current surge in the global prevalence of obesity reflects the failure of mechanisms that regulate body weight to cope with environments that promote overeating and discourage physical activity. Yet, within any obesity-promoting environment there is considerable variation among individuals regarding their susceptibility to weight gain. (1)Some become obese despite a continuous struggle not to, whereas others stay lean without conscious control. Such variations in the propensity for weight gain may reflect varying susceptibilities to overeating or to a sedentary life-style. But we also know from overfeeding experiments that humans vary in their capacity to resist weight gain because of varying abilities to convert food directly into heat, a process called (2)diet-induced thermogenesis(DIT). The magnitude of this apparent "energy wastage" is determined by the genetic makeup of the individual and by the composition of their diet. (3)Identifying components of the body's autoregulatory system that induce DIT will help us to understand the genetic and metabolic basis of susceptibility to obesity, and to develop better anti-obesity therapies.

　　The sympathetic nervous system(SNS) influences many physiological functions—ranging from body temperature homeostasis to blood pressure regulation—by releasing the neurotransmitter norepinephrine, which acts upon α-and β-adrenergic receptors. Ever since researchers began to study DIT in the 1960s, they have tried to implicate the SNS in the regulation of this process. Possible SNS involvement in thermogenesis is suggested by the ability of norepinephrine to control biochemical pathways that lead either to an increase in consumption of ATP (for example, through pumping ions across membranes or recycling substrates) or to an increased rate of mitochondrial oxidation (with poor coupling of ATP synthesis leading to increased heat production).

(4) But it was not until Landsberg *et al.* demonstrated that SNS activity in a variety of tissues is boosted during overfeeding and decreased during starvation (a state of energy conservation) that the SNS was cast as the efferent system linking diet and thermogenesis. Finally, with their contribution in this issue, Bachman *et al.* provide (5) direct evidence that the SNS is indeed the prime mediator of DIT. These authors reveal that mice lacking all three β-adrenergic receptors ($β_1AR$, $β_2AR$, $β_3AR$) cannot increase thermogenesis and become massively obese during overfeeding. In contrast to these "β-less" mice, wild-type mice are able to resist obesity during overfeeding by activating DIT.

（出典：Abdul G. Dulloo, *A Sympathetic Defense Against Obesity*, Science, **297**:780-781, 2002（一部改変））

《語注》
obesity：肥満
propensity：生まれつきの性質
homeostasis：恒常性
norepinephrine：ノルエピネフリン（ノルアドレナリンの別名）
adrenergic receptor：アドレナリン受容体
susceptibility：感受性
sympathetic nervous system：交感神経
neurotransmitter：神経伝達物質
efferent：遠心性

問1　下線(1), (3), (4)を和訳しなさい．

問2　下線(2)のDITとは何か．30字以内で説明しなさい．

問3　下線(5) "direct evidence" となる実験結果について125字以内で具体的に説明しなさい．

【問題 2】 以下の英文を読んで設問に答えなさい．

愛媛大学　平成16年　380語　30分

　The role of diagnostic X-rays has evolved from classic conventional radiography and uniform thick slice CT to highly specialized imaging, which has the potential to reduce the overall radiation exposure of individuals undergoing the examination and has better diagnostic accuracy. However, there is no threshold of radiation dose under which the absence of any cancer risk is proven. On the other hand, there are no reliable data proving that radiation doses as used in diagnostic X-rays do induce cancer.

　In today's Lancet, Amy Berrington de González and Sarah Darby use cancer-rate data from survivors of the Japanese atomic bombings as a model to study the risk of cancer from diagnostic X-rays.（中略）

　The Japanese survival data are the best available because there are no other data showing the effect of ionising radiation on a large human population; but the data have limitations. One limitation is that the survivors were not only directly exposed with γ rays from the bomb detonations but also with β radiation, and, most importantly, α radiation from contaminated food, water, and dust in the air. This additional exposure will not occur in patients undergoing radiological examinations but contributes to the morbidity and mortality of the atomic bomb survivors. Additionally the γ rays to which the atomic bomb survivors were exposed were of a different energy spectrum from that used for diagnostic X-ray. Without better data, however, it is probably adequate to use the Japanese data. But these additional concerns should be taken seriously and the derived numbers for the incidence of cancer caused by X-rays should be critically assessed in future investigations, because the cancer risk is probably overestimated with use of the Japanese data.

（中略）

　Berrington de González and Darby did not assess the indications or benefits achieved for patients in X-ray examinations. Benefits include the earlier detection of cancers by radiological examinations and the possibility of early treatment, which probably allows more cure of cancers than radiological exposure is able to cause.

　A general goal must be to avoid unnecessary X-ray procedures. Up to 30% of chest X-rays may not be indicated; unnecessary CT examinations can lengthen hospital stay as well as causing radiation exposure. In everyday practice, those ordering radiological procedures should think carefully about the benefit for and the

risk to their patients for each examination.
（出典：Peter Herzog, Christina T. Rieger, *Risk of cancer from diagnostic X-rays*, The Lancet, **363**:9406, 2004）

《語注》
diagnostic：診断上の　　　　　　　　　morbidity：罹患
CT（Computed Tomography）：X線コンピューター断層撮影装置

問1　下線の部分を和訳しなさい．

問2　発癌リスクの推定に用いたデータの問題点をどのように指摘しているかを150字以内で答えなさい．

問3　日常診察において診断用の放射線被爆と発癌のリスクに関してどのように考えるべきか，100字以内でまとめなさい．

問4　以下の日本語を英訳しなさい．
　放射線の人体に及ぼす影響には，放射線皮膚炎や放射線白内障のようにある一定（閾値）以上の被爆により発現する確定的影響と，発癌や奇形といった少量であってもリスクを増加させる確率的影響との2つがある．
　（参照　放射線皮膚炎：radiation dermatitis，放射線白内障：radiation cataracta，確定的影響：deterministic effect，奇形：anomaly，確率的影響：stochastic effect）

【問題 3】 次の文章を読み，下記の問題に答えなさい．
鹿児島大学　平成23年　1402語　45分

　　Biophysicist David Brenner was in his 40s when an older colleague in New York City, a prominent pediatric radiologist, mentioned in conversation something Brenner couldn't shake: Far too many children, the pediatrician felt, were getting computed tomography (CT) scans for ailments, such as suspected appendicitis, that used to be diagnosed easily by ultrasound or even observation. Cells in children, already more vulnerable because they divide faster than those of adults, have more time to turn cancerous after the initial damage from radiation. And a single CT scan delivers a lot of it, the equivalent of dozens to a few hundred chest x-rays. A concern about the CT boom, planted 11 years ago, began to grow.

　　Brenner now directs Columbia University's Center for Radiological Research, where he focuses on exactly how radiation damage leads to cancer. He seems an unlikely candidate for ① a troublemaker, a passionate Beatles fan who speaks so quietly, he's sometimes hard to hear. Yet he's become one of the most insistent voices in an imbroglio that is roiling radiologists, medical physicists, and the general public over the rising and largely unregulated use of CT scans, and whether the technology can, in same（筆者注：「some」の間違いであろう）cases, cause more harm than good.

　　Brenner hails from Liverpool, U.K., and his Upper West Side apartment shows it: A large black-and-white poster of a young and pensive George Harrison hangs above the sofa, and a plastic John Lennon figurine from the movie Yellow Submarine crouches next to the stereo. Settled on a couch in his living room, he explains how he moved to the center of the CT storm.

　　"What I thought I could contribute to this discussion was to provide some quantitative estimates of what the risks [of CT scans] actually were," he says. These risks are surprisingly unclear, given how old and how commonly used the technology is. Brenner found that each CT scan gives a patient a very small chance of developing cancer. With hundreds of thousands of children getting CT scans every year, that small individual risk balloons into a pressing public health concern, Brenner concluded.

Many radiologists and medical physicists strongly disagree. For a single CT scan, they say, there's no hard evidence of any raised cancer risk. Nor do they think that thousands of small, potential risks add up to a large public health problem. Furthermore, they say, the dearth of evidence makes it difficult to assess how low is low enough. But even the skeptics favor managing potential CT risks, if for no other reason than to reassure patients. That's one of the aims behind a summit co-sponsored by the U.S. National Institute of Biomedical Imaging and Bioengineering in Bethesda, Maryland, that ends this week. Researchers there discussed standardizing protocols, estimating doses, and dose-saving technologies.

As the debate rages, the number of CT scans administered continues to soar. In 1980, 3 million scans were given in the United States. In 2006, the number was about 67 million. It shows no sign of slowing down.

How small a risk?

CT scans deliver the same type of radiation as an x-ray machine, but much more of it. As the patient moves through the scanner, x-ray beams and detectors revolve around the bed. The body's tissues absorb radiation to varying degrees, and what gets through creates slice-by-slice, incredibly detailed images of the body part being scanned. Crafting this picture comes with potential risks. The chromosomes of a healthy cell are tangled in a "spaghetti-like formation," Brenner explains. If radiation breaks up the chromosomes, the strands can usually repair themselves. Sometimes, though, the wrong ends meet up, scrambling the genetic information and leaving behind a premalignant cell that can bloom into cancer.

Eleven years ago, when Brenner first began considering ② children's CT risks, he needed two pieces of information: the radiation delivered by a single CT scan, and the probability that a dose to a given organ would produce a fatal cancer there. For the first, he used a 1989 British survey of CT use in adults to estimate the dose children experience. For the second, Brenner turned to "the only quantitative tool we had and still have," he says: risk calculations of radiation-induced cancer in survivors of the atomic bombings of Hiroshima and Nagasaki. The most recent were published in a report by the National Research Council in 1990 and updated in 2006.

Because data on atomic bomb survivors who had died of cancer were more robust, Brenner focused on fatal cancers. The chance of a child someday dying of cancer from one CT scan was small—on the order of one in 1000, Brenner found. But given that about 600,000 abdominal and head CT scans were performed yearly on children at the time that Brenner did his research, he and his colleagues estimated that 500 of those children might end up dying later on in life of cancer caused by the scan. Meanwhile, the total number of children who would get cancer from CT scans would be about twice that, he estimated. Brenner published his results in early 2001 in the American Journal of Roentgenology.

The paper was a sensation. "CT scans in children linked to cancer," blared a headline in USA Today. Brenner's use of the atomic bomb data raised "the ire of lots of people" in the medical physics and radiology communities, he says. They criticized him for extrapolating from the risks associated with extraordinarily high doses from an atomic bomb.

But Brenner says he didn't need to extrapolate. In Hiroshima, "as you go further and further away [from the epicenter], doses get less and less, so eventually you get to a region where the doses are actually comparable to a CT scan," he says. Brenner based his risk estimates on a cadre of about 30,000 survivors whose doses were in the range of 5 to 100 millisieverts, equivalent to one or two CT scans, he says.

Keith Strauss, a medical physicist at Children's Hospital Boston, clearly remembers the day in 2001 when Brenner's research was described in USA Today. The article "ruined my life for 2 weeks," Strauss said in an interview in Philadelphia last July, at the annual meeting of the American Association of Physicists in Medicine (AAPM). His patients' parents were suddenly full of worries and questions about their children's scans.

By 2010, concerns about CT scans and cancer were getting plenty of attention; AAPM sessions on dose reduction were packed. Brenner had first sounded the alarm, but now others were raising concerns, too. In March 2009, the National Council on Radiation Protection and Measurements (NCRP) reported that, in 2006, CT radiation alone contributed 24% of the U.S. population's radiation dose. In 1980, that number was 0.4%.

"The NCRP report was really the crucial one [that showed] the dramatic increase in the level of exposure," says Amy Berrington de González, a radiation epidemiologist at the National Cancer Institute in Bethesda, who was not part of the NCRP panel. In late 2009, Berrington de González and her colleagues published a paper in Archives of Internal Medicine estimating that the approximately 70 million scans performed in the United States in 2007 would lead to about 29,000 new cancers.

③ There's still a great deal of controversy, however, about how dangerous CT scans really are. Cynthia McCollough, a medical physicist at the Mayo Clinic in Rochester, Minnesota, is skeptical that there's any evidence for the risks Brenner and Berrington de González have reported. To her, the research on doses in the CT range do not show any meaningful biological effect. Some studies, she says, suggest that low doses can even be protective against cancer, similar to how the weakened virus in a flu vaccine helps the body fight off that year's flu. As for whether patients getting multiple scans should worry more, cells can repair themselves between scans, she says, so the damage shouldn't be cumulative. And like others, she's leery of looking at survivors of an atomic bomb blast.

At last November's meeting of the Radiological Society of North America (RSNA) in Chicago, Illinois, McCollough and Brenner engaged in a public debate over whether cancer risks should be taken into account when ordering CT scans. At the end, the audience was polled and was evenly split. Brenner has his estimates, but "no one," says James Brink, the chair of diagnostic radiology at Yale University School of Medicine, "has conclusively shown that medical radiation has caused cancer."

(出典：Lauren Schenkman, *Second Thoughts About CT Imaging*, Science, **331**, 1002-1004, 2011)

《語注》
biophysicist：生(物)物理学者
pediatrician：小児科医
computed tomography：コンピュータX線断層写真撮影
appendicitis：虫垂炎
vulnerable：傷つきやすい
radiological：放射線(医)学の
roil：いらだたせる
pediatric：小児科医の
radiologist：放射線学者
ultrasound：超音波を用いた診断
cancerous：癌に罹った
imbroglio：ごたごた
skeptic：懐疑論者

premalignant：前がん性の
roentgenology：X線学
epicenter：爆心地
millisieverts：ミリシーベルト（電離放射線の線量当量の国際基本単位）
epidemiologist：疫学者
ire：怒り
extrapolate：推定する
cadre：一員
leery：凝っている

問1　下線部①の意味するところを，本文に即して日本語で150字以内にまとめなさい．

問2　下線部②について，Brennerが根拠とした事実を本文に即して日本語で200字以内にまとめなさい．

問3　下線部③は具体的にどのような意見があるか，本文に即して日本語で250字以内にまとめなさい．

【問題 4】 次の英文を読んで，下の問いに日本語で答えなさい．

新潟大学　平成19年　785語　20分

　　In the movie thriller Memento, the principal character, Leonard, can remember everything that happened before his head injury on the night his wife was attacked, but anyone he meets or anything he has done since that fateful night simply vanishes. He has lost the ability to convert short-term memory into long-term memory. Leonard is driven to find his wife's killer and avenge her death, but trapped permanently in the present, he must resort to tattooing the clues of his investigation all over his body.

　　(a)That disturbing story was inspired by the real case history of a patient known in the medical literature only as "HM." When HM was nine years old, a head injury in a bicycle accident left him with debilitating epilepsy. To relieve his seizures that could not be controlled in any other way, surgeons removed parts of HM's hippocampus and adjoining brain regions. The operation succeeded in reducing the brain seizures but inadvertently severed the mysterious link between short-term and long-term memory. Information destined for what is known as declarative memory—people, places, events—must pass through the hippocampus before being recorded in the cerebral cortex. Thus, memories from long ago that were already stored in HM's brain remained clear, but all his experiences of the present soon faded into nothing. HM saw his doctor on a monthly basis, but at each visit it was as if the two had never met.

　　This transition from the present mental experience to an enduring memory has long fascinated neuroscientists. A person's name when you are first introduced is stored in short-term memory and may be gone within a few minutes. But some information, like your best friend's name, is converted into long-term memory and can persist a lifetime. The mechanism by which the brain preserves certain moments and allows others to fade has recently become clearer, but first neuroscientists had to resolve (b)a central paradox.

　　Both long- and short-term memories arise from the connections between neurons, at points of contact called synapses, where one neuron's signal-emitting extension, called an axon, meets any of an adjacent neuron's dozens of signal-receiving fingers, called dendrites. When a short-term memory is created, stimulation of the synapse is enough to temporarily "strengthen," or sensitize, it to subsequent signals. For a long-term memory, the synapse strengthening becomes permanent. Scientists have been aware since the 1960s, however, that this requires genes in the neuron's nucleus to activate, initiating the production of proteins.

Memory researchers have puzzled over how gene activity deep in the cell nucleus could govern activities at faraway synapses. How does a gene "know" when to strengthen a synapse permanently and when to let insignificant moments fade unrecorded? And how do the proteins encoded by the gene "know" which of thousands of synapses to strengthen? The same questions have implications for understanding fetal brain development, a time when the brain is deciding which synaptic connections to keep and which to discard. In studying that phenomenon, my lab came up with an intriguing solution to one of these mysteries of memory. And just like Dorothy, we realized that the answer was there all the time.

Early molecular biologists discovered that genes play a role in the conversion of a memory from short- to long-term. Their experiments with animals trained to perform simple tasks demonstrated that learning required new proteins to be synthesized in the brain within minutes of training, or else the memory would be lost.

(c)For a protein to be produced, a stretch of DNA inside the cell nucleus must be transcribed into a portable form called messenger RNA (mRNA), which then travels out to the place where cellular machinery translates its encoded instructions into a protein. These researchers had found that blocking the transcription of DNA into mRNA or the translation of mRNA into a protein would impede long-term memory formation but that short-term memory was unaffected.

Because one neuron can form tens of thousands of synaptic connections and there could not possibly be a gene dedicated to each one, cellular neuroscientists sought to explain how the cell nucleus was controlling the strength of these individual connections. They theorized that an unknown signaling molecule must be generated by a synapse when it was sufficiently stimulated. (d)With its connection temporarily strengthened, this synapse could hold the memory for a short time while the signaling molecule departed, wending its way to the nucleus of the nerve cell. There this messenger molecule would activate appropriate genes needed to synthesize proteins that would permanently strengthen the synaptic connection. Yet a second problem was how this protein, once it was manufactured in the cell body of the neuron, could then find the one synapse among thousands that had called for it.

(出典：R. Douglas Fields, *Making Memories Stick*, Scientific American, February, 2005)
Reproduced with permission. Copyright © 2005 Scientific American, Inc. All rights reserved.

《語注》
hippocampus：(脳の)海馬　　　　　cerebral cortex：大脳皮質
neuron：ニューロン，神経単位　　　synapse：シナプス
axon：軸索　　　　　　　　　　　dendrite：樹状突起
nucleus：(細胞の)核

問1　(a)の内容を簡潔に説明しなさい．
　　　(人名については本文中のまま表記してよい)

問2　(b)の内容を簡潔に説明しなさい．

問3　(c)を和訳しなさい．
　　　('DNA'，'mRNA' についてはそのまま使用してよい)

問4　(d)を和訳しなさい．

1.2 要約問題

【問題 5】 次の英文を 200 字程度の和文で要約せよ.

東京工業大学大学院　平成20年　377語　20分

　　Microbes run the world. It's that simple. Although we can't usually see them, microbes are essential for every part of human life—indeed all life on Earth. Every process in the biosphere is touched by the seemingly endless capacity of microbes to transform the world around them. The chemical cycles that convert the key elements of life – carbon, nitrogen, oxygen, and sulfur—into biologically accessible forms are largely directed by and dependent on microbes. All plants and animals have closely associated microbial communities that make necessary nutrients, metals, and vitamins available to their hosts. Through fermentation and other natural processes, microbes create or add value to many foods that are staples of the human diet. We depend on microbes to remediate toxins in the environment —both the ones that are produced naturally and the ones that are the byproducts of human activities, such as oil and chemical spills. The microbes associated with the human body in the intestine and mouth enable us to extract energy from food that we could not digest without them and protect us against disease causing agents.

　　These functions are conducted within complex communities—intricate, balanced, and integrated entities that adapt swiftly and flexibly to environmental change. But historically, the study of microbes has focused on single species in pure culture, so understanding of these complex communities lags behind understanding of their individual members. We know enough, however, to confirm that microbes, as communities, are key players in maintaining environmental stability.

　　By making microbes visible, the invention of microscopes in the late 18th century made us aware of their existence. The development of laboratory cultivation methods in the middle 1800s taught us how a few microbes make their livings as individuals, and the molecular biology and genomics revolutions of the last half of the 20th century united this physiological knowledge with a thorough understanding of its underlying genetic basis. Thus, almost all knowledge about microbes is largely "laboratory knowledge", attained in the unusual and unnatural circumstances of growing them optimally in artificial media in pure culture without ecological context. The science of metagenomics, only a few years old, will make it possible to investigate microbes in their natural environments, the complex communities in which they normally live. It will bring about a transformation in biology, medicine, ecology, and biotechnology that may be as profound as that initiated by the invention of the microscope.

(出典：Committee on Metagenomics, *The New Science of Metagenomics: Revealing the Secrets of Our Microbial Planet*, The National Academies Press, 2007)

《語注》
staple：必需品
intestine：腸
intricate：複雑な
spill：流出
digest：消化する
integrated entity：統合された存在

【問題6】次の文章を読んで，設問に答えなさい．

鹿児島大学　平成20年　814語　30 ～ 35分

　　DNA is hip. At least that's what the new breed of genetic marketers would like you to believe. Last week, Navigenics, a California Web-based company, launched its $2,500 personalized DNA test—spit into a test tube and we'll tell you your risk for heart attack and other conditions—at a storefront in New York's trendy SoHo neighborhood. Computers, set against an orange and pink double helix, showed off Navigenics's Web site. Waiters circulated with pink cocktails—past a woman in a fur shrug over here, past Al Gore, a friend of the company (and partner in a firm that's invested in Navigenics), over there. Tony Bonidy, 60, from Pittsburgh, attended the much-publicized kickoff and wants to get himself and his family tested. "This is incredible," he said.

　　It's been 55 years since Watson and Crick defined the structure of DNA. Today, DNA is defining us. Most of the 1,100 genetic tests on the market are for rare single-gene diseases, like cystic fibrosis. But now, DNA-testing companies say they can scan our genomes and tell us our potential risk for diabetes, Alzheimer's and other common chronic conditions. Our DNA, once a mystery, is suddenly a commodity, and some two dozen businesses are competing for it in cyberspace. In January, another new company, 23andMe, handed out 1,000 free tests at the World Economic Forum in Davos, then boasted on its blog, The Spittoon, that "scholars, celebs and politicos swarmed" its booth. Featured photos: Naomi Campbell showing off her test kit, New York Times columnist Thomas Friedman spitting into his.

　　But what's the science behind all the hype? Direct-to-consumer (DTC) genetic-testing companies differ in their wares and the stringency of the research they rely on. DNA Direct, launched in 2005, offers diagnostic tests for individual disorders like hemochromatosis, or iron overload ($199). Most customers have family histories and want to know if they're at risk too, says CEO Ryan Phelan. Other companies sweep the genome more broadly. Navigenics scans nearly 1 million DNA snippets, then homes in on markers associated with 18 conditions, including multiple sclerosis and lupus—all of them influenced by multiple genes, many still unidentified. And then there's the entertaining stuff—23andMe ($999) and competitor deCODE Genetics ($985) provide gene tests not just for health conditions (alcohol flush reaction and lactose intolerance included), but for genetic ancestry as well.

　　With each new marketing push comes new criticism. Michael Watson, of the

American College of Medical Genetics, says DNA testing doesn't belong in virtual clinics: "We're very concerned about the trivialization of genetics." One key issue is regulation. While the government mandates that genetic tests be performed in certified labs, not all are, and there's little to no oversight of a given test's accuracy or clinical usefulness. The individual gene variants linked to complex conditions may have only a modest effect on risk. And most DTC companies don't take lifestyle issues, like smoking, or family history into account, even though both can bump the odds up or down. There's plenty of debate, too, over the usefulness of information that can't be translated into action. Yes, you can cut out the fat and start jogging if your diabetes risk appears to be higher, but why pay hundreds of dollars to get that message?

Dr. Thomas Morgan, of the Washington University School of Medicine in St. Louis, worries that the business is getting ahead of the science. While researchers have clearly identified a chromosomal region linked to heart attack, for example, no single gene—including some being analyzed by DTC companies—stands out as the smoking gun. And undiscovered genes may turn out to be major risk factors. The result, says Morgan: "I might scare myself or reassure myself falsely based on the very limited knowledge that we have."

Market share, however, will not come to those who wait. "It's a matter of getting the field jump-started," says Dietrich Stephan, one of two scientists who founded Navigenics. The company, which offers genetic counseling, says its goal is improving health. Knowing your personal risk can lead to action, says CEO Mari Baker. Her genome scan found markers for celiac disease, a gluten allergy. A subsequent blood test came back positive. Now she avoids wheat, rye and barley. Most results won't lead to such clear-cut outcomes, though, and a recent report found that physicians are unprepared to deal with this wave of genetic information. Navigenics is offering a course for docs on Medscape to help fill the gap—a great way to market its product, too.

Andrew Meyer, 23, has caught the genome bug. Last December, he asked for donations on his blog, Buzzyeah.com, because he didn't have the cash. The $10s, $20s and $50s poured in. Meyer is still analyzing his 23andMe report, which he is sharing with the public. His motivation? "I'm really curious," he says. One day, no doubt, there'll be genetic tests for that, too.

(出典：Claudia Kalb, *May We Scan Your Genome?*, Newsweek, **21**, 2008)
"From Newsweek 4/12 ⓒ 2008 The Newsweek/Daily Beast Company LLC. All rights reserved."

Used by permission and protected by the Copyright Laws of the United States. The printing, copying, redistribution, or retransmission of the Material without express written permission is prohibited."

《語注》
cystic fibrosis：嚢胞性線維症　　　　　　diabetes：糖尿病
Alzheimer's：アルツハイマー症　　　　　　hype：誇大広告
hemochromatosis：血色素症，ヘモクロマトーシス
iron overload：鉄過剰症　　　　　　　　　multiple sclerosis：多発性硬化症
lupus：エリテマトーデス　　　　　　　　　trivialization：平凡化，軽視
celiac disease：セリアック病

問　この文章は新しい遺伝子検査の登場とその問題点に関する記事である．新しい遺伝子検査はどのような問題点があると論じているか．本文に即して日本語で300字以内にまとめなさい．

1.3 選択式問題

【問題 7】 次の文章を読んで設問に答えよ.
高知大学　平成17年　915語　35分

　The idea that physicians and nurses should wash their hands before treating a new patient is a relatively recent innovation. Ignaz Semmelweis, the man credited with making hand washing a standard part of medical practice, lived and practiced medicine in the mid-1800s. Although he was not the first physician to make the connection between contaminated hands and the spread of disease by physicians to their patients, he was the first to prove that proper disinfection of hands could dramatically reduce hospital-acquired infections. Semmelweis had noted that two maternity wards in the Vienna Lying-in Hospital had very different mortality rates. In one, the death rate due to childbed fever (a common cause of death in women of the period) was about 3%, whereas in the second ward it was over 10%. This fact was well known to women entering the hospital, who considered assignment to the second ward to be a virtual (①). Both wards were equally crowded, with three patients sharing each bed, the sick mixed indiscriminately with the well, and both wards contained women of similar socioeconomic status. The only difference was that women in the first ward were attended by student midwives, and the women in the second ward were attended by male medical students. Semmelweis noted that the medical students frequently went to the ward to make vaginal examinations after dissecting cadavers, some of whom had died of childbed fever. The student midwives in the first ward were not only not dissecting cadavers but were expected to pay more attention to physical cleanliness than the medical students. Semmelweis deduced that the medical students were transmitting childbed fever (which we now know is caused most frequently by the bacterium *Streptococcus pyogenes*) to their patients because they failed to cleanse their hands properly. In 1846, he began to require that all midwives and medical students wash their hands with a chlorine solution before examining patients. The death rate in both wards promptly dropped to 1%, something the women who came to the ward appreciated but Semmelweis's male detractors did not. Semmelweis's discovery remained controversial for many years and it was only in the early 1900s that hand washing was universally accepted as an essential medical practice.

Today, proper disinfection of hands is one of the most basic and firmly entrenched of clinical procedures, especially for surgeons. Nonetheless, the advent of antibiotics and the consequent decrease in deaths due to hospital-acquired infections has led some surgeons to neglect this important practice. A particularly dramatic example of this was provided by a surgeon in a large northeastern U.S. hospital who started bypassing the rigorous surgical scrub procedure because he was troubled by dermatitis on his hands. He trusted to the two pairs of surgical gloves, which were commonly worn during operations. But tiny holes in gloves can be made by contact with sharp objects or bone fragments. Also, the surgeon was using mineral oil to ease the irritation to his hands, and mineral oil (②) the integrity of surgical gloves. This physician managed to contaminate heart valve implants in a number of patients with *Staphylococcus epidermidis* before he was identified as the source of the outbreak. *S. epidermidis* is commonly found as part of the resident microbiota of the skin, where it is not normally pathogenic, but it can cause infections if introduced into the body through wounds. Infections of heart valve implants usually cannot be treated effectively with a simple course of antibiotics, not only because of the high resistance level of *S. epidermidis* strains but also because of the formation of bacterial biofilms that are more resistant to antibiotics than individual bacteria. Thus, the patients with the infected valves had to endure a second operation to remove and replace the infected valve, not to mention additional damage to the heart due to the infection.

As is evident from the date on the reference cited at the end of this section, this case occurred in the 1980s. Does this mean that such cases have ceased to occur? Not at all. This case was used because it is a classic example of the hand-washing problem, but there have been many other cases since. The difference between the 1980s and the first decade in the 21st century is that today the surgeon in this case would probably have been discovered before he infected so many people, (③) . But the attitude and behavior that sparked this sorry episode were still rampant in many hospitals in the 1980s.

The silver lining in (1) this particularly black cloud is that the accountants for the insurance agencies have finally figured out how much the lack of hand washing and improper use of gloves (④), and they are mounting increasingly vigorous campaigns in favor of hand washing and against health care workers who ignore these simple but effective precautions. In fact, relatives of hospital patients are being urged to question unhygienic practices they witness. The lawyers are circling. Who

knows? It might even become safe to enter a hospital in the coming years.
（出典：Abigail A. Salyers and Dixie D. Whitt, *Bacterial Pathogenesis, A Molecular Approach, 2nd ed.*, Amer Society for Microbiology, 2002（一部改変））

問1　次のa～dの記述のうち，本文の内容について正しいものの組み合わせを1～16から選べ．

a. Semmelweisは医師の汚染された手指が患者に病気を広めている可能性にはじめて気づいた人物である．
b. 医学生は助産師学生よりも手指の清潔を心がけていた．
c. たとえ手術用手袋を着用していても，外科手術を行っている医師の手指の常在菌が患部へ移行することが起こりうる．
d. 21世紀になって，患者を診察する前に手洗いをしないような医師はいなくなった．

1. a　　2. b　　3. c　　4. d　　5. a, b　　6. a, c　　7. a, d　　8. b, c　　9. b, d
10. c, d　　11. a, b, c　　12. a, b, d　　13. a, c, d　　14. b, c, d　　15. a, b, c, d
16. すべて誤り

問2　次のa～eの記述のうち，Semmelweisが産褥熱（childbed fever）と手洗いの関係に気づいた理由と関係の深いものはどれか．最も適切な組み合わせを1～16から選べ．

a. 病棟により死亡率に違いがあった．
b. 病棟により入院患者の社会的地位に違いがあった．
c. 病棟により患者を担当する学生の専攻が異なった．
d. 病棟によりベッドあたりの患者数に有意な差があった．
e. 病棟により患者担当学生の妊婦診察の頻度が違った．

1. a　　2. b　　3. c　　4. d　　5. e　　6. a, b　　7. a, c　　8. a, d　　9. a, e
10. b, c　　11. b, d　　12. b, e　　13. c, d　　14. c, e　　15. d, e　　16. すべて誤り

問3　本文中の（①），（②），（④）に入る適切な語句の組み合わせはどれか．1〜9から選べ．

	①	②	④
a	death sentence	underlines	is costing them
b	death sentence	underlines	is economical
c	death sentence	undermines	is costing them
d	death sentence	undermines	is economical
e	favorable news	underlines	is costing them
f	favorable news	underlines	is economical
g	favorable news	undermines	is costing them
h	favorable news	undermines	is economical

1. a　2. b　3. c　4. d　5. e　6. f　7. g　8. h　9. すべて誤り

問4　次のa〜eの記述のうち，（③）に入る適切な文節はどれか．1〜6から選べ．

a. because infectious disease surveillance systems in hospitals have improved
b. because novel antibiotics to treat the infectious disease were developed
c. because the vaccine for preventing the infectious disease was developed
d. because novel disinfectants have succeeded in the effective eradication of the bacteria from surgeons' hands
e. because awareness of the importance of hand washing has increased in hospitals

1. a　2. b　3. c　4. d　5. e　6. すべて誤り

問5　次のa〜eの記述のうち，下線部(1)の "this particularly black cloud" の意味として適切なものはどれか．1〜6から選べ．

a. *S. epidermidis* 等の常在菌が皮膚に存在していること．
b. 抗生物質で治療不能な細菌による院内感染症が激増していること．
c. 病院での院内感染の実態調査が不十分であること．
d. 手洗いの重要性が近年でさえ医師たちに十分認識されていなかったこと．
e. 弁護士らが医療過誤を起こした医師に対して訴訟を起こそうとしていること．

1. a　2. b　3. c　4. d　5. e　6. すべて誤り

1.4 英作文

【問題 8】 次の英文を読み，以下の設問に答えなさい．解答はすべて解答用紙の指定欄に記入しなさい．

旭川医科大学　平成 17 年　1727 語　90 分

　You are a third-year medical student on the last day of a clinical rotation. You have seen a total of 2 lumbar punctures. Just before you enter a patient's room and leaving you no time to respond, your attending physician says, "I'm going to introduce you as 'doctor.' It makes it easier for the patient and you need to do a spinal tap before you finish your rotation." As you enter the room, the attending physician tells the patient, "This is Dr [Smith], who will be doing your lumbar puncture." The attending physician and the patient both look at you expectantly. What do you do? What are the ethical and professional considerations that would guide your response?

　In their study of third-and fourth-year medical students, Beatty and Lewis found that 100 percent of students surveyed had experienced being introduced to patients as "doctor" by members of the medical team. When attending physicians introduce medical students as "doctors" to facilitate their gaining experience with procedures such as spinal taps, medical students must quickly determine if this deception is justified and if not, whether, how, and when to correct it.

　The requirement of obtaining a patient's informed consent prior to any substantial intervention is intended to respect patient autonomy, minimize risk, and prevent exploitation and injustice. To this end, most legal jurisdictions require that physicians disclose what a reasonable person in similar circumstances would find relevant to the decision at hand. Presumably, novices have a higher rate of complications when performing new procedures than do more experienced clinicians. Therefore, most, if not all, reasonable persons would wish to know the true status and qualifications of individuals involved in their care and, in particular, of those individuals who wish to perform fairly risky interventions for the first time. With regard to spinal taps specifically, 2 separate studies found that more than 80 percent of patients would want to know the experience level of the person doing the tap. (A)Since reasonable patients clearly find this information material to their decision, true informed consent cannot be obtained without disclosing the true status of medical students as students, not doctors.

Circumventing informed consent requires strong justification, and few exemptions exist. Nevertheless, (B)3 common justifications are given for deceiving or not otherwise disclosing to patients the status and experience levels of medical students performing procedures. They are: (1)consent to be treated by medical students is implied by allowing oneself to be admitted to an academic medical center, (2)knowing the status of medical students performing procedures would cause patients unnecessary stress and nervousness, and (3) societal necessity; ie, if patients were told and refused treatment from students, future patients would suffer at the hands of inadequately trained physicians. Let's look at each of these.

Consent to admission into a teaching hospital does not imply consent to the involvement of medical students in the provision of care to all patients. Most patients, and particularly poor or uninsured patients, have little choice about which hospitals they are admitted to. Some patients are not even aware they are in a teaching hospital. Moreover, if patients truly consented to receive care from medical students upon admission to a teaching hospital, there would be no need to deceptively refer to medical students as "doctors."

While it is true that informing patients that medical students are performing procedures for the first time may make patients anxious, it is also true that most patients who later discover that they were not told or were deceived about a medical student's involvement, become upset. The stress and distrust that results when this is revealed may be worse than the stress caused by the disclosure of a students' role prior to a procedure. Furthermore, full disclosure is necessary for patients to exercise their right, as recognized in the American Medical Association's *Code of Medical Ethics*, to determine whether or not to participate in a student's medical education. If a student's role is disclosed prior to a procedure, some patients may refuse the student's participation. To some degree this is desirable and would serve to demonstrate that medicine is meeting its obligation to foster patient autonomy by allowing patients to make informed decisions about their care.

But what if all patients refused and medical education could not proceed? While this is a legitimate concern, evidence suggests that, when asked, many patients are willing to allow medical students to participate in aspects of their care. In their survey of 100 internal medicine outpatients, Ubel and Silver-Isenstadt found that less than half of the patients would "probably" or "definitely" refuse to allow students to perform even the more sensitive exams (eg, rectal or pelvic exams). They found that the majority of patients were willing to interact with students in a wide variety of clinical settings. With regard to spinal taps, specifically, Williams and Fost found that 52 percent of those surveyed would be willing to be the subject of a student's first tap, while Ubel and Silver-Isenstadt report that 66 percent would definitely not allow a medical student to perform a spinal tap. The consent rate was considerably lower in an emergency department setting where direct faculty supervision was not guaranteed. Taking these studies into account, approximately one-third or more of patients may be willing to allow students to perform spinal taps in non-emergency settings. Although this rate of patient participation may hinder training, it is not unmanageable. Moreover, some of the patients' apprehension regarding spinal taps, may be due to a commonly held, but false, belief that spinal taps carry a high risk of paralysis. Education about the procedure may result in greater patient willingness to participate. Still, more research is needed. All 3 studies involved hypothetical situations and no study has looked at patients who actually need spinal taps to determine the impact of full disclosure on whether or not patients ultimately allow medical students to perform spinal taps.

Furthermore, medical students are not the only novices in hospitals. Residents, fellows, and even attending physicians must inevitably perform procedures for the first time as new technologies and interventions are developed. If research showed that the number of patients willing to receive care from novices, at any professional level, was too few to adequately and efficiently train physicians, then the "social necessity" justification would have to be revisited and the burden of medical education would have to be distributed to all members of society. Poor and uninsured patients in public hospitals, where students and residents supply a greater proportion of patient care, should not unwillingly be subject to greater risk and discomfort from first-time procedures than private patients.

(C) What then is a medical student to do when an attending physician introduces her as a "doctor" in order to secure her an opportunity to perform an important yet moderately risky procedure? To resolve this question the medical student must examine her role and obligations within 2 complex relationships: the mentor-student relationship and the doctor-patient relationship.

The Hippocratic Oath helps illustrate the duties inherent in these 2 relationships. The oath calls on students "to hold [their] teacher in this art equal to [their] own parents". By equating preceptors to parents, the oath reminds us of the authority of preceptors over their students and of students' responsibility to respect this authority. More generally, the oath is used to remind students and physicians of their responsibility, within the doctor-patient relationship, to act in their patients' best interests and above all do no harm.

In the case of a spinal tap or other procedure of moderate risk, the student's responsibilities and allegiances are in conflict. To show concern and respect for the patient's welfare and autonomy, the student ought to reveal her true status and allow the patient to make an informed decision about the student's participation. The greater the potential for harm, the greater the responsibility to be completely forthright. However, if the student is to respect the authority of the attending physician, then she should not correct the attending physician. Complicating matters, the student's evaluation may depend, at least in part, on how well the student meets this latter responsibility. The student must also consider the consequences her actions may have on the relationship between the patient and the attending physician.

The central element of all these relationships is trust, and honesty is a critical part of developing trusting relationships. To preserve these vital partnerships, the student must act in a way that maximizes or preserves the trust between all parties to the greatest degree. This will depend heavily on the particular circumstances of the situation.

One way for the medical student to preserve or maximize trust is to excuse herself from the room and ask the attending physician to step out with her. Privately the student may begin by thanking the attending for helping to create learning opportunities for her and express her desire to learn new procedures. This helps demonstrate from the start that the student values this relationship, is eager to learn, and respects and appreciates the attending physician. The student should then express her concern that, should the patient later learn, say by noting it on the student's name badge, that the "doctor" is really a student, the patient may lose trust in them. This allies the student and the attending physician over a shared concern in securing the trust of the patient. Not passing judgment on the attending physician's actions maximizes the likelihood that the attending physician will respond positively and minimizes the risk to the student. It sets the stage for a discussion in which the student and attending physician can negotiate how to approach future patients and ethically learn new procedures. Although the medical student may lose out on the opportunity to perform a spinal tap on this particular patient, she may lessen the moral burden all medical students carry as they attempt to learn new procedures on unsuspecting patients.

Granted not all physicians will respond positively, and just how far a student must push the issue depends on the potential harms to the patient. Certainly students are not required to sacrifice their careers to prevent minimal harms. Although the approach I have proposed may be uncomfortable for some students, it poses minimal risk and therefore, the students owe it to their patients, attending physicians, and themselves to attempt to clarify their student status.

(出典：William Martinez, *Trust Me. I'm a Doctor,* Virtual Mentor, Vol **7**, Number 4, 2005)

問1 次の (1) ～ (3) の設問に日本語で答えなさい.
(1) 下線部 (A) を日本語に訳しなさい.
(2) ①下線部 (B) の 3 common justifications とは何か, 本文の内容に即して述べなさい.
   ② 3 common justifications に対する筆者の見解を述べなさい.
(3) 下線部 (C) に対して筆者はどのように答えているか, まとめなさい.

問2 Read the following, and answer in English.

In this essay it mentions that in the Hippocratic Oath doctors should 'do no harm'. However, with the rapid progression of medical science the situation has become more complicated. Do you think doctors can practice medicine and carry out research without violating this part of the Hippocratic Oath?

Please write your opinions on this referring to one or some of the controversial areas in modern medicine listed below:
abortion, cloning, euthanasia, gene therapy, genetic testing, organ transplants, physician-assisted suicide etc.

【問題 9】 次の文章の下線部を英訳せよ．
浜松医科大学　平成15年　20～30分

　科学とは何かを知ろうとすれば，科学でないもの，たとえば疑似科学，あるいは似非（えせ）科学との区別は何かを明確に出来ることが大切である．つまり，前節に述べたように，対立する概念とのちがいを明確にするのである．そのような観点からすれば，科学は誰にも理解され，科学的実験は誰がおこなっても同じ結果が再現できることが，必須の条件であるといえるだろう．つまり，科学においては客観性が保証されねばならないわけである．そのためには，科学の論文はまちがいのない理論にしたがって議論と推論をおこない，観測や実験などによってその結果が実証できるものでなければならない．実験においては実験の材料や条件，そして実験の結果が正確に記述されて，誰もがこれを追試（追いかけて実験すること）できねばならないわけである．

(出典：長尾真著『「わかる」とは何か』(岩波新書))

【問題 10】 以下の文章を英訳せよ.
島根大学　平成22年　30分

1) 電子顕微鏡の開発によって，科学者達たちは標準的な光学顕微鏡を使って見ていたのと比べて，自然の世界のより奥深い部分を見ることができるようになった．

2) インフルエンザはインフルエンザウイルスによって引き起こされる伝染性の呼吸器系疾患であり，軽度から重篤な病気を引き起こし，時には死に至ることもある．

3) ある研究によれば，肺炎，下痢，マラリア，敗血症といった感染症は，世界で毎年8,800,000人いる，5歳未満の子供の死亡の3分の2以上の原因を占めている．

4) 血液が動脈から静脈へ移動する際，毛細血管で濾過される体液の10%は，生命維持に必要なたんぱく質と一緒に，体の組織内に溜まってしまう．この体液の損失はリンパ系が適切に機能しないと，即座に生命に危険を及ぼすことになるだろう．

第2章
テーマ別問題演習

2.1 医師と患者の関係

【問題 11】 次の英文を読み，問に答えなさい．

新潟大学　平成21年　801語　35分

Improved health, functional and emotional status

　　Good doctor patient communication has been shown to have a positive impact on a number of health outcomes in previous studies. a) In a study that explored the effects of communication-skills training on the process and outcome of care associated with patient's emotional distress, improvement in physicians' communication skills was shown to be associated with a reduction in emotional distress in patients (Roter et al, 1995). In a review of 21 randomised controlled trials and analytic studies on the effects of physician-patient communication on patient health outcomes, the quality of communication in both history taking and discussion of the management plan was found to be associated with health outcomes (Stewart, 1995). Better doctor patient communication was shown to be associated with better emotional and physical health, higher symptom resolution, and better control of chronic diseases that included better blood pressure, blood glucose and pain control. More recently, in a study conducted on 39 randomly selected family physician offices and 315 patients, b) Stewart et al (2000) showed that the degree of patient-centred communication was associated with less discomfort, less concern and better mental health in patients. Moreover, in terms of reduction of utilisation of health services, it was shown that patients who perceived that their visits had been patient centred received fewer diagnostic tests and referrals in the subsequent months. In another study that investigated physician interaction styles and perceived health services quality by patients, Flocke et al (2003) performed a cross-sectional study looking at 2881 patient visits of 138 family doctors and categorised physicians' interaction styles into 4 categories: person-focused, biopsychosocial, biomedical, and high physician control by the use of a primary care instrument. They showed that physicians with a personfocused interaction style with patients were associated with the highest reported quality of care by patients, while physicians with the high control styles were associated with the lowest reported quality of care.

Compliance with medical treatment

Low compliance with prescribed medical interventions is an important problem in medical practice and it is associated with substantial medical cost including increased hospital admissions. It also creates an ongoing frustration to health care providers (Melnikow, 1994). Finding ways to improve compliance is of interest to both health service administrators and physicians. To this end, c) the doctor patient relationship may have an important role to play. It has been shown that doctor's attitude towards his patients, his ability to elicit and respect the patients' concerns, the provision of appropriate information and the demonstration of empathy and the development of patient trust are the key determinants of good compliance with medical treatments in patients (DiMatteo, 1994; Safran et al, 1998). Furthermore, training doctors to improve their communication skills could potentially be cost-effective as it increases compliance which in turn improves the overall health of patients (Cegala, 2000).

Improved Patient Satisfaction

Effective doctor patient communication is shown to be highly correlated with patient satisfaction with health care services. In a study (Jackson, 2001) involving 500 patients who were seen by 38 primary care clinicians for physical symptoms, aspects of patient doctor communication such as "receiving an explanation of the symptom cause, likely duration, and lack of unmet expectations" were found to be the key predictors of patient satisfaction. In another review of 17 studies (Lewin, 2002) by the Cochran Library that was conducted to study the effects of interventions directed at health care providers to promote patient-centred care, training health care providers in patient-centred approaches was shown to impact positively on patient satisfaction with care. d) Patient satisfaction is an important area that deserves our attention because dissatisfaction with health care services can result in litigation against doctors by patients, unnecessary health care expenditure due to repeated visits, both could be very costly for the health care system.

Improved clinician satisfaction

Although much emphasis has been put on the importance of effective communication and good doctor patient relationship in affecting patient health outcomes and satisfaction, e)physician satisfaction with their professional life can also be an important determinant of a good doctor patient relationship. In a study conducted in the outpatient division of a teaching hospital, it was shown that physician's satisfaction with their professional life was associated with greater patient trust and confidence in their primary care physicians (Grembowski D, 2004). It seems that physicians who are themselves more satisfied may be better able to address patient's concern (Hall,1990). It has been suggested that physicians who are satisfied with their professional life may have more positive effect, which may in turn affect their communication with patients which then affect patient satisfaction (Hall, 1988). The exact mechanism for how physician satisfaction is related to patient satisfaction is not known, although authors have suggested that both could be affected by a third confounding factor such as one's personality attribute that relates to both empathic and communication skills. How these are related await further research (Roter, 1997).

(出典: Samuel YS Wong, Albert Lee, *Communication skills and Doctor Patient Relationship*, The Hong Kong Medical Diary, Vol. **11**, No.3, 2006)

問1　a) を和訳しなさい．

問2　b) の結果を本文に即して説明しなさい．

問3　c) はどのような役割か．本文に即して説明しなさい．

問4　d) を和訳しなさい．

問5　e) がもたらす効果を本文に即して説明しなさい．

【問題 12】 次の記事を読み，文末の注釈を参考に各問いについて最もふさわしい答えをア〜エの選択肢の中から1つ選び，解答欄の記号にマークしなさい．

東海大学医学部一般編入試験　平成23年　774語　25分

The dramatic legacy of one woman's immortal cells

In today's medical environment, where paperwork-overwhelmed patients often feel they have to sign their rights away just to have a simple blood test, it's hard to imagine a time when the concepts of informed consent and bioethics didn't exist. For those of us born in the post-Civil Rights era, it's also difficult to conceive of race-based hospital exclusion or separate wards for white and "colored" patients. But that was the reality in 1951, when a poor, uneducated black woman named Henrietta Lacks sought treatment for what turned out to be cervical cancer [*1], and a biopsy [*2] taken without her consent changed the course of medical history.

Lacks didn't know she was making an (1)unparalleled contribution to medical research when a doctor at Johns Hopkins in Baltimore took a tissue sample as she was being treated. She died a few months later, but her cells went on to become seemingly (2)immortal workhorses that replicated themselves in culture and sustained scientific inquiry for decades. Lacks' family wouldn't find out about her prolific cells and the medical advances and industry profits (3)they generated for more than 20 years after her death, writes Rebecca Skloot, a science writer and author of the new book

The Immortal Life of Henrietta Lacks.

(4)The HeLa cells, as they're known, have been used to develop the polio and human papilloma virus (HPV) [*3] vaccines, sent into space to determine the effect of zero gravity on human tissue, and were among the first ever cloned and gene-mapped. And in a cruel irony, they also led to some important cancer medications, Skloot noted during our recent conversation. HeLa cells are still grown and used around the world today.

Hope and despair

(5)The book is a fascinating medical mystery—scientists still haven't pinpointed why Lacks' cells are able to survive and thrive in the lab when others die off within months—but it's foremost a haunting family narrative and a reminder that health care is intensely personal. For years, Lacks' husband and five children (6)fielded calls about Henrietta's cells, but scientists didn't clearly explain who was using them and for what purposes.

Her cells launched a multibillion-dollar human biological-materials industry and a few con artists and (7)crooked scientists pursued research on the family for their own gain, but Henrietta Lacks' descendants couldn't afford health insurance or basic medical care. It's no surprise that her relatives were consumed with anger and mistrust by the time Skloot arrived on the scene in the late 1990s with the goal of telling Lacks' story.

Not only did Henrietta Lacks die young, but she knew tragedy well before she got sick. Her second child Elsie was born epileptic[*4] and deaf and went to live at what was then called the Hospital for the Negro Insane, where the book says she was most likely subjected to cruel experimentation and died in 1955 at the age of 15.

Elsie's younger sister Deborah, a key figure in the book, was as determined to find out what happened to (8)her institutionalized sibling as she was to learn more about her mother. In Skloot's hands, the Lacks family's poignant story unfolds like a novel, with Deborah vacillating between desperately wanting to know the truth and fighting the urge to give up the search for it because it proved so painful. Deborah's own health suffers as she delves deeper into the details.

To help Lacks' descendants with scholarships and health insurance, Skloot has set up the Henrietta Lacks Foundation, open to anyone who wants to contribute. The family also may gain by selling their story to Hollywood.

Evolving standards of informed consent

Where does the legacy of Henrietta Lacks leave patients today with regard to informed consent?

Certain practices—such as naming cell lines after people, as scientists did with HeLa cells—no longer happen, Skloot said. Cells taken today are stripped of personal identity.

"What happened to the family in the '70s—researchers coming to them and taking samples specifically for research—does require consent now," Skloot said. "It would violate federal law to do otherwise."

But the idea of informed consent gets murky when it comes to the cells collected during routine blood tests and biopsies.

"We sign forms that say 'You can dispose of my tissues any way you see fit. You can use them in research,' " Skloot said. "As long as your name is removed from them and the researcher hasn't had firsthand contact with you, that doesn't require consent. And often those are used in research and commercialized and there's a lot of debate going on right now about how to handle that."

(出典：Gerencherk, *The dramatic legacy of one woman's immortal cells*, The Wall Street Journal, April 29, 2010)

《語注》
*1 cervical cancer：子宮頸がん　　　　　*2　biopsy：生体組織検査
*3 human papilloma virus（HPV）：ヒト乳頭腫ウイルス
*4 epileptic：てんかん（性）の

(1) The underlined word <u>unparalleled</u> means
ア．equal.　　イ．unprecedented.　　ウ．enduring.　　エ．unpredictable.

(2) The underlined word <u>immortal</u> means
ア．undying.　　イ．energetic.　　ウ．short-lived.　　エ．standard.

(3) The underlined word <u>they</u> refers to
ア．the medical advances.　　イ．the Lacks family.
ウ．the industry profits.　　　エ．Lacks' prolific cells.

(4) Scientist have used <u>the HeLa cells</u>
ア．to inform Lacks' family that Henrietta is still alive.
イ．to experience zero gravity.
ウ．to promote the idea of informed consent among the general public.
エ．to discover how to treat polio and cancer.

(5) <u>The book is a fascinating medical mystery</u> for scientists because
ア．they have not figured out why Lacks' cells are kept alive outside the body while others are not.
イ．they cannot understand why the Lacks family refuses to make HeLa cells available for scientific research.
ウ．HeLa cells have led many of them to work in the world of biomedical research.
エ．only a limited number of them are allowed to have access to HeLa cells.

(6) The underlined word fielded means
ア．made.　　イ．rejected.　　ウ．answered.　　エ．missed.

(7) The underlined word crooked means
ア．leading.　　イ．reliable.　　ウ．clear-headed.　　エ．dishonest.

(8) The underlined word her institutionalized sibling refers to
ア．Henrietta Lacks.　　イ．Elsie Lacks.　　ウ．Rebecca Skloot.
エ．Deborah Lacks.

(9) Deborah felt so shocked because
ア．her family agreed to turn her mother's story into a movie.
イ．she was discouraged from talking with the author of the book.
ウ．she faced the fact about her sister's tragic life while learning about her mother.
エ．she could not find a sponsor to establish the Henrietta Lacks Foundation.

(10) As a result of the Henrietta Lacks case, which of the following is NOT true?
ア．Scientists should secure consent before they take tissue samples for research under federal law.
イ．The rules about informed consent are unclear regarding cells taken during routine blood tests.
ウ．Cell lines are still named after the people who provided the tissues.
エ．Persons must give consent before tissue samples are taken.

2.2 最新医療技術

【問題 13】 次の英文を読んで以下の問に答えなさい.
千葉大学　平成19年　1231語　90分

　In 1984 and 1985, I was among a dozen or so researchers who proposed a Human Genome Project (HGP) to read, for the first time, the entire instruction book for making and maintaining a human being contained within our DNA. The project's goal was to produce one full human genome sequence for $3 billion between 1990 and 2005.

　We managed to finish the easiest 93 percent a few years early and to leave a legacy of useful technologies and methods. Their ongoing refinement has brought the street price of a human genome sequence accurate enough to be useful down to about $20 million today. Still, that rate means large-scale genetic sequencing is mostly confined to dedicated sequencing centers and reserved for big, expensive research projects.

　The "$1,000 genome"(1) has become shorthand for the promise of DNA-sequencing capability made so affordable that individuals might think the once-in-a-lifetime expenditure to have a full personal genome sequence read to a disk for doctors to reference is worthwhile. Cheap sequencing technology will also make that information more meaningful by multiplying the number of researchers able to study genomes and the number of genomes they can compare to understand variations among individuals in both sickness and health.

　"Human" genomics extends beyond humans, as well, to an environment full of pathogens, allergens and beneficial microbes in our food and our bodies. Many people attend to weather maps; perhaps we might one day benefit from daily pathogen and allergen maps. The rapidly growing fields of nanotechnology and industrial biotechnology, too, might accelerate their mining of biomes for new "smart" materials and microbes that can be harnessed for manufacturing or bioremediation of pollution.

　The barrier to these applications and many more, including those we have yet to imagine, remains cost. Two National Institutes of Health (NIH) (2) funding programs for "Revolutionary Genome Sequencing Technologies" challenge scientists to achieve a $100,000 human genome by 2009 and a $1,000 genome by

2014. An X Prize–style cash reward for the first group to attain such benchmarks is also a possibility. And these goals are already close. A survey of the new approaches in development for reading genomes illustrates the potential for breakthroughs that could produce a $20,000 human genome as soon as four years from now—and brings to light some considerations that will arise once it arrives.

Lowering Cost

Evaluating the next-generation sequencing systems against one another and against the Sanger method illustrates some of the factors that will influence their usefulness. For example, two research groups, my own at Harvard and one from 454 Life Sciences, recently published peer reviewed descriptions of genome-scale sequencing projects that allow for a direct comparison.

My colleagues and I described a sequencing-by-ligation system that used polony bead amplification of the template DNA and a common digital microscope to read fluorescent signals. The 454 group used a similar oil-emulsion PCR for amplification followed by base-extension sequencing with pyrophosphate detection in an array of wells. Both groups read about the same amount of sequence, 30 million base pairs, in each sequencing run. Our system read about 400 base pairs a second, whereas 454 read 1,700 a second. Sequencing usually involves performing multiple runs to produce a more accurate consensus sequence. With 43-times coverage (43 ×)—that is, 43 runs per base—of the target genome, 454 achieved accuracy of one error per 2,500 base pairs. The Harvard group had less than one error per three million base pairs with 7 × coverage. To handle templates, both teams employed capture beads, whose size affects the amount of expensive reagents consumed. Our beads were one micron in diameter, whereas 454 used 28-micron beads in 75-picoliter wells.

The best available electrophoresis-based sequencing methods average 150 base pairs per dollar for "finished" sequence. The 454 group did not publish a project cost, but the Harvard team's finished sequence cost of 1,400 base pairs per $1 represents a ninefold reduction in price.

These and other new techniques are expected very soon to bring the cost of sequencing the six billion base pairs of a personal genome down to $100,000. For any next-generation sequencing method, pushing costs still lower will depend on a few fundamental factors. Now that automation is commonplace in all systems, the biggest expenditures are for chemical reagents and equipment. Miniaturization has already reduced reagent use relative to conventional Sanger reactions one billionfold from microliters to femtoliters.

Accuracy requirements will also be a function of the applications. Diagnostic uses might demand a reduction in error rates below the current HGP standard of 0.01 percent, because that still permits 600,000 errors per human genome. At the other end of the spectrum, high-error-rate (4 percent) random sampling of the genome has proved useful for discovery and classification of various RNA and tissue types. A similar "shotgun" strategy is applied in ecological sampling, where as few as 20 base pairs are sufficient to identify an organism in an ecosystem.

Raising Value

Beyond developing these new sequencing technologies, we have much work to do in a short amount of time to get ready for the advent of low-cost genome reading. Software will be needed to process sequence information so that it is manageable by doctors, for example. They will need a method to derive an individualized priority list for each patient of the top 10 or so genetic variations likely to be important. Equally essential will be assessing the effects of widespread access to this technology on people.

From its outset, the HGP established a $10-million-a-year program to study and address the ethical, legal and social issues that would be raised by human genome sequencing. Participants in the effort agreed to make all our data publicly available with unprecedented speed—within one week of discovery—and we rose to fend off attempts to commercialize human nature. Special care was also taken to protect the anonymity of the public genomes (the "human genome" we produced is a mosaic of several people's chromosomes). But many of the really big questions remain, such as how to ensure privacy and fairness in the use of personal genetic information by scientists, insurers, employers, courts, schools, adoption agencies, the government, or individuals making clinical and reproductive decisions.

These difficult and important questions need to be researched as rigorously as the technological and biological discovery aspects of human genomics.

The personal genome project

Every baby born in the U.S. today is tested for at least one genetic disease, phenylketonuria, before he or she leaves the hospital. Certain lung cancer patients are tested for variations in a gene called EGFR to see if they are likely to respond to the drug Iressa. Genetic tests indicating how a patient will metabolize other drugs are increasingly used to determine the drugs' dosage. Beginnings of the personalized medicine that will be possible with low-cost personal genomes can already be glimpsed, and demand for it is growing.

　　Beyond health concerns, we also want to know our genealogy. How closely are we related to Genghis Khan or to each other? We want to know what interaction of genes with other genes and with the environment shapes our faces, our bodies, and our dispositions. Thousands or millions of data sets comprising individuals' whole genome and phenome — the traits that result from instructions encoded in the genome — will make it possible to start unraveling some of those complex pathways.

(出典:George M. Church, *Genomes for All*, Scientific American, January, 2006)
Reproduced with permission. Copyright © 2006 Scientific American, Inc. All rights reserved.

《語注》
43-times coverage:43回の繰り返し
454 Life Sciences:(米国) 454ライフサイエンスズ社(高速DNA配列決定法を開発する会社)
adoption:養子縁組　　　　　　　　　allergen:アレルゲン
biomes:バイオーム(気候によって分けられた生態系に含まれる生物の集団)
bioremediaton:微生物や菌類や植物,あるいはそれらの酵素を用いて有害物質で汚染された自然環境(土壌汚染の状態)を,有害物質を含まない元の状態に戻す処理のこと.
disposition:(生来の)気質　　　　　　fend:対抗する,払いのける
fluorescent:蛍光の　　　　　　　　　genealogy:系統学(家系学,経歴学)
Genghis Khan:チンギス・ハーン(成吉思汗)　Ligation:ライゲーション,連結反応
Microbe:微生物
National Institutes of Health (NIH):(米国)国立衛生研究所
pathogen:病原体
phenome:個体の表現形質,フェノタイプの集合概念(生命がもつ1セットの遺伝子集合がゲノム)
phenylketonuria:フェニルケトン尿症
polony bead:ポリメラーゼコロニー (polymerase colony, a small colony of DNA)
　　Polonies are discrete clonal amplifications of a single DNA molecule, grown on a solid-phase surface.
pyrophosphate detection:ピロリン酸塩検出法(1つの塩基が相補鎖に付け加えられたときに放出される分子で,発光タンパク質と化学反応して光る)
Sanger method:サンガー法(DNA配列決定の方法)
sequence:配列(タンパク質中のアミノ酸の,核酸の残基の),配列を決定する
unprecedented:先例のない,空前の

問1　ヒトゲノムDNA構造を読解するのに，(1) 当初，どれくらいの期間にいくらの費用をかけたのか，(2) 最近では全構造を読解するのに費用はいくらかかるか，併せて140字以内の日本語で説明しなさい．

問2　下線部(1)の「＄1,000 genome」という表現で何を言おうとしているか，その意味とそれが現実になったらどのような波及効果が期待されるか，具体例を本文の内容にそって240字以内の日本語で説明しなさい．

問3　下線部(2)のNational Institutes of Health（NIH）が資金援助する2つのプログラムはどのようなものか，140字以内の日本語で説明しなさい．

問4　DNAの構造決定に利用されている方法で最も費用のかかるところはどの部分か，また，構造決定のコストを下げるためにどのような工夫がなされているか，本文の内容にそって140字以内の日本語で説明しなさい．

問5　遺伝子検査は，社会にどのように応用され，貢献しているのか，具体的な例を本文の内容にそって合計300字以内の日本語で説明しなさい．

問6　個人の遺伝情報が入手可能になることにより，どのような社会的な問題点が生じるか，本文の内容と自分の考えを300字以内の日本語で述べなさい．

【問題 14】 以下の文章を読んで設問に答えなさい。なお、一部の語句には文末に注を付してあります。

千葉大学　平成23年　1281語　60分

　On June 26, 2007, Wendy Chung, director of clinical genetics at Columbia University, drove to the New York City borough of Queens with a delicate request for the Croatian matriarchs of a star-crossed family. She asked the two sisters, one 82 and the other 89, if they would donate some of their skin cells for an ambitious, highly uncertain experiment that, if it succeeded, promised a double payoff. One, it might accelerate the search for treatments for the incurable disease that ran in their family. Two, it might establish a valuable new use for stem cells: unspecialized cells able to (1a) give rise to many different kinds of cells in the body.

　It took Chung just a couple minutes to perform the actual "punch biopsy"— two quick nips of (1b) flesh, each three millimeters in diameter, from the inner arm. Eventually the sisters' cells, along with skin samples from dozens of other ALS patients and healthy volunteers who similarly donated bits of tissue were chemically induced to become a form of stem cell known as an induced pluripotent stem cell and were then reprogrammed to become nerve cells. Specifically, they were induced to become motor neurons, the nerve cells that directly or indirectly control the muscles of the body and are adversely affected by ALS. The resulting tissue cultures exhibited the same molecular defects that gave rise to ALS in their human donors. In other words, the investigators had, ▢3a▢ an astonishing extent, re-created the disease in a petri dish.

　The stem cells used in these studies should not be confused with embryonic stem cells—the kind derived from early embryos. A dozen years ago James A. Thomson and his colleagues at the University of Wisconsin–Madison (2a) electrified the world with the news that they had created human embryonic stem cells in a lab for the first time. These primordial cells had the biological endurance to renew themselves forever and the versatility to turn into any cell type in the body.

　But two harsh realities awaited. First, a loud public debate over the ethics of stem cell science politicized the science and slowed research; the technology posed moral questions because human embryos had to be destroyed to harvest the embryonic stem cells. That debate culminated in President George W. Bush's announcement in August 2001 that the National Institutes of Health would restrict funding support to research using only a few existing embryonic stem cell lines, which effectively impeded the generation of additional stem cells, including the disease-specific cell lines.   3b   response, prominent research groups at Harvard, Columbia and Stanford universities, along with patient advocacy groups such as Project ALS and the New York Stem Cell Foundation, created separate, "nonpresidential" labs to pursue research with private funding.

The second problem was scientific. As Valerie Estess, scientific director of Project ALS, recalls it, there was a mad rush to test the idea that specialized cells derived from stem cells could simply be transplanted into sick people (or animals) as cellular therapies to cure a host of diseases. "The big dream," she explains, "was to derive motor neurons from stem cells, and then you would put them in the brain or spinal cord, and the patients would just get up and start dancing the Watusi." But it did not work out that way in repeated animal experiments. "From beginning to end," Estess says, "these experiments were failures."

In 2002 Thomas M. Jessell, Hynek Wichterle and their team at Columbia published a landmark paper in the journal Cell, spelling out the ingredients and procedure for nudging embryonic stem cells down a biological pathway to form motor neurons. One researcher who saw in that work promise   3c   a different use of stem cells was Rubin. Elfin and enthusiastic, Rubin had trained in neuroscience and served as research and chief scientific officer of a Massachusetts biotech company called Curis. He realized that creating a disease in a dish offered a potentially revolutionary way to discover drugs. And unlike a lot of academic scientists, he knew something about drug discovery.

After hearing the results of Jessell and Wichterle's research, Rubin drafted a business plan for a new kind of stem cell institute, "one that focused," he says, "not on cell therapy—which all stem cell biologists were interested in—but on using stem cells to discover drugs." At the time, venture capitalists wanted nothing to do with the idea. So Rubin (2b) <u>nursed the idea</u> along at Curis, working on spinal muscular atrophy, a childhood motor neuron disease that has a similar pathology to ALS. When Curis decided to drop the project in 2006, he quit biotech and moved to the Harvard Stem Cell Institute to pursue the disease-in-a-dish idea.

Shortly afterward, a Japanese biologist named Shinya Yamanaka disclosed a technique that would ultimately transform both stem cell biology and stem cell politics. At a scientific meeting at Whistler, B.C., in March 2006, the Kyoto University scientist described a procedure by which biologists could take ordinary adult mammalian cells and "reprogram" them. In essence, Yamanaka had biochemically reset the adult cells back to an embryoniclike or stemlike state ⬜4⬜. He called the cells "induced pluripotent stem cells," or iPS cells. A year later both Yamanaka and Wisconsin's Thomson separately reported that they had created iPS cells from human tissue.

One of the people sitting in the audience that day in Whistler was Eggan, who was a cellular reprogramming expert at Harvard. In fact, he had already (2c) embarked on his own version of the disease-in-a-dish idea, launching several projects to take an adult cell and biochemically (1c) coax it back into an embryolike state, allow it to replicate, and harvest stem cells from the resulting colony. He was trying to make embryolike cells the "old-fashioned" way, however, ⬜3d⬜ applying the same cloning technique that produced Dolly the sheep. Eggan would take the nucleus out of an adult cell, such as a skin cell, and implant it into an unfertilized egg whose own nucleus had been removed. Cloning, however, was terribly inefficient and also terribly controversial if you planned to reprogram human cells— ⬜5⬜ because you had to find women willing to donate their egg cells for the procedure.

Using Yamanaka's approach, however, Eggan and his team finally got the iPS technique to work in a test run with human cells in the summer of 2007. (6) Everything else was already in place to try the disease-in-a-dish concept. Chung and her Columbia colleagues, for example, had collected cells from the two Croatian sisters and other ALS patients in anticipation that they would be used in Eggan's cloning experiments. With private funding, Project ALS had created a special laboratory near Columbia where researchers had been stockpiling cell lines from patients (including the elderly sisters) for months. Suddenly, the iPS approach offered a better chance of success. "That was complete kismet, that we had begun to collect human skin cells with a very different experiment in mind," says Estess of Project ALS.

(7) The headliner among all those first ALS cell lines was the one from the younger, sicker Croatian sister, identified as patient A29. The skin cells of both sisters were successfully reprogrammed into nerve cells, but the age and degree of illness in patient A29 demonstrated that the iPS technique could be used to create cells that reflected a serious, lifelong disease. "We chose those samples because those were the oldest people in our study, " Eggan says. "We wanted to prove the point that you could reprogram cells even from a very, very, very, very old person who'd been sick for some length of time. They were a special case."

Reproduced with permission. Copyright © 2011 Scientific American, Inc. All rights reserved.
（出典：Stephen S. Hall, *Diseases in a Dish*: *Stem Cells for Drug Discovery*, Scientific American, March 2011, p41-45）

《語注》
borough：治村（町）　　　　　　　　　　matriarch：女家長
star-crossed：不幸な　　　　　　　　　　incurable：治らない
Amyotrophic Lateral Sclerosis（ALS）：筋萎縮性側索硬化症
pluripotent：多能性の，多分化能の　　　petri dish：細胞培養用の容器
stem cells：幹細胞　　　　　　　　　　　embryonic：胎児（由来）の
primordial cells：始原生殖細胞　　　　　versatility：多能性，多分化能
culminate：頂点に達する　　　　　　　　transplant：移植する
the Watusi：アメリカ合衆国で流行した踊りの一種
nudge：やんわりと押す　　　　　　　　　elfin：魅力的な
venture capitalists：ベンチャービジネスに投資する人
pathology：病理，病態　　　　　　　　　unfertilized：未受精の
stockpile：備蓄する　　　　　　　　　　headliner：立役者
kismet：宿命，運命

問1　本文中の (1a) (1b) (1c) の下線部と同様な意味を表す別な英単語1語を，本文中に使われている単語から選んで，解答欄に記入しなさい．

問2　本文中の (2a) (2b) (3c) の下線部を5～15字の日本語に訳しなさい．

問3　本文中の 3a 3b 3c 3d に入る適切な前置詞を解答欄に記入しなさい．

問4　以下の英単語を並び替えて， 4 に当てはまる正しい英文とし，解答欄に記入しなさい．
（use　destroy　to　without　needing　embryo　or　an）

問5　 5 に当てはまる，文脈に対し最も適切な語句を以下の選択肢から1つ選んで，解答欄に番号で答えなさい．
　　1　at least
　　2　at most
　　3　but
　　4　not least
　　5　only

問6　下線(6)は何を意味しているか，60〜120字の日本語で具体的に説明しなさい．

(注) 問6から問10の解答の際，人名，地名，固有名詞，ALS，iPSは英語のままでよい．英文字についても1字，1マスを使用すること．
　以下の単語についてはカタカナで表現してもよい．
　　cloning（クローニング）　　　　　　colony（コロニー）
　　Croatian（クロアチアの）　　　　　　reprogram（リプログラム）
　　reprogramming（リプログラミング）

問7　下線(7)に書かれているpatient A29由来の細胞がheadlinerである理由を60〜120字の日本語で具体的に説明しなさい．

問8　stem cell（幹細胞）の従来考えられていた利用法とRubinが考えた新しい利用法を対比して，80〜160字の日本語で説明しなさい．

問9　James A. Thomsonが発表したhuman embryonic stem cellの研究において，本文に書かれている2つの問題点とは何か．80〜160字の日本語で説明しなさい．

問10　YamanakaのiPS細胞の手法を知る前のEgganはどのようにしてadult cellをembryonic cellに変えようとしていたか，本文中に書かれている具体的な方法について50〜100字の日本語で説明しなさい．

2.3 現代において問題となっている疾患

【問題 15】 以下の文章は, Thompson & Thompson, "Genetics in Medicine 7th ed."の中のものです. 以下の文章を読んでから, 質問に答えなさい.

愛媛大学 平成21年 451語 30分

　　In clinical practice, the chief significance of genetics is in elucidating the role of genetic variation and mutation in the etiology of a large number of disorders. (1)Virtually any disease is the result of the combined action of genes and environment, but the relative role of the genetic component may be large or small. Among disorders caused wholly or partly by genetic factors, three main types are recognized: chromosome disorders, single-gene disorders, and multifactorial disorders.

　　(2)In chromosome disorders, the defect is due not to a single mistake in the genetic blueprint but to an excess or a deficiency of the genes contained in whole chromosomes or chromosome segments. For example, the presence of an extra copy of one chromosome, chromosome 21, produces a specific disorder, Down syndrome, even though no individual gene on the chromosome is abnormal. As a group, chromosome disorders are quite common, affecting about 7 per 1000 liveborn infants and accounting for about half of all spontaneous first-trimester abortions.

　　A) Single-gene defects are caused by individual mutant genes. The mutation may be present on only one chromosome of a pair (matched with a normal allele on the homologous chromosome) or on both chromosomes of the pair. In a few cases, the mutation is in the mitochondrial rather than the nuclear genome. In any case, the cause is a critical error in the genetic information carried by a single gene. Single-gene disorders usually exhibit obvious and characteristic pedigree patterns. Most such defects are rare, with a frequency that may be as high as 1 in 500 but is usually much less. Although individually rare, as a group single-gene disorders are responsible for a significant proportion of disease and death. Taking the population as a whole, single-gene disorders affect 2 % of the population sometime over an entire life span. In a population study of more than 1 million live births, the incidence of serious singlegene disorders in the pediatric population was estimated to be 0.36 %; among hospitalized children, 6% to 8% probably have single-gene disorders.

(B) inheritance is responsible for a number of developmental disorders resulting in congenital malformations and for many common disorders of adult life. There appears to be no single error in the genetic information in many of these conditions. Rather, the disease is the result of a combination of small variations in genes that together can produce or predispose to a serious defect, often in concert with environmental factors. Multifactorial disorders tend to recur in families but do not show the characteristic pedigree patterns of single-gene traits. Estimates of the impact of multifactorial disease range from 5% in the pediatric population to more than 60 % in the entire population.

(出典：Thompson & Thompson, *Genetics in Medicine, 7th ed.*, Saunders, 2007)

問1　下線(1)(2)を日本語に訳しなさい(それぞれ100字程度).

問2　下線Aの段落を要約し，日本語120字以内で記しなさい.

問3　Bに入る適切な単語を文章の中から選んで答えなさい.

問4　この文章全体にふさわしい表題は何か．日本語20字以内で記しなさい.

【問題 16】 以下の英文を読んで問いに答えなさい.
愛媛大学　平成23年　671語　30分

For type 2 diabetes and obesity, the discovery of causal genes has followed 1)three main waves. The first wave consisted of family-based linkage analyses and focused candidate-gene studies. These proved effective in identifying genes responsible for extreme forms of early-onset disease segregating as single-gene (mendelian) disorders. Genes underlying several distinct, familial forms of nonautoimmune diabetes—including maturity-onset diabetes of the young, mitochondrial diabetes with deafness, and neonatal diabetes—were characterized. Similar approaches revealed mutations in genes responsible for rare forms of severe childhood obesity, including the genes encoding leptin, the leptin receptor, and proopiomelanocortin. These discoveries have provided insights into processes critical for the maintenance of normal glucose homeostasis and energy balance and clues to the inner workings of the pancreatic beta cell and hypothalamus. For many families, this information has led to improved diagnostic and therapeutic options.

Attempts to apply similar approaches to families in which either common forms of diabetes or obesity is segregating have proved to be largely unrewarding, and the second wave of discovery involved a switch to tests of association. Although 2)intrinsically more powerful than linkage analysis, association analysis suffers from the disadvantage that the signal can be detected only if one examines the causal variant itself or a nearby marker with which it is tightly correlated. 3)Until the advent of methods that enabled genomewide surveys of association, researchers were therefore obliged to direct their attention to specific candidate variants or genes of interest. In retrospect, it is obvious that most such studies were seriously underpowered or focused on inappropriate candidates. Nevertheless, by accruing data over the course of multiple studies, some genuine susceptibility variants were identified. Common coding variants in *PPARG* and *KCNJ11* (each of which encodes a protein that acts as a target for classes of therapeutic agents widely used in diabetes management) were shown to have modest effects on the risk of type 2 diabetes. Resequencing of the gene encoding the melanocortin-4 receptor (MC4R) resulted in the identification of low-frequency coding variants that explain approximately 2 to 3% of cases of severe obesity.

The third, and most successful, wave of discovery has been driven by systematic, large-scale surveys of association between common DNA sequence variants and disease. The first demonstration that unbiased discovery efforts could reveal new insights into the pathogenesis of type 2 diabetes resulted from identification of the association between type 2 diabetes and variants within *TCF7L2* (encoding transcription factor 7–like 2, a protein not previously identified as a biologic candidate). *TCF7L2* has now been shown to modulate pancreatic islet function.

  4) <u>The number of loci for which there is convincing evidence that they confer susceptibility to type 2 diabetes started to grow in early 2007 with the publication of the first genomewide association studies.</u> Together, these studies revealed six new associations, including variants near *CDKAL1*, *CDKN2A*, and *CDKN2B* (which encode putative or known regulators of cyclin-dependent kinases) and *HHEX* (which is transcribed into a homeobox protein implicated in beta-cell development). Typically each copy of a susceptibility allele at one of these loci is associated with a 15 to 20% increase in the risk of diabetes. Since then, the dominant approach to discovery has involved ever-larger aggregations of genomewide association data from multiple samples so as to improve the power to identify variants of modest effect: these studies have revealed more than 20 additional confirmed signals of susceptibility to type 2 diabetes. Though early studies were restricted to samples obtained from persons of European descent, genomewide association analyses conducted in other ethnic groups are now emerging. The current total of approximately 40 confirmed type 2 diabetes loci includes variants in or near *WFS1* (wolframin) and the hepatocyte nuclear factors *HNF1A* and *HNF1B* (genes that also harbor rare mutations responsible for monogenic forms of diabetes); the melatonin-receptor gene *MTNR1B* (which highlights the link between circadian and metabolic regulation); and 5)<u>*IRS1* (encoding insulin-receptor substrate 1), one of a limited number of type 2 diabetes loci with a primary effect on insulin action rather than on secretion.</u>

(出典：Mark I. McCarthy, *Genomics, Type 2 Diabetes, and Obesity*, NEJM, **363**, 2339, 2010)

《語注》
diabetes：糖尿病
nonautoimmune：非自己免疫性
neonatal：新生児の
hypothalamus：視床下部
mendelian：メンデルの法則の
maturity-onset：成人発症の
pancreatic：膵臓の
resequencing：再度の塩基配列解読

問1 1) three main waves は何を意味するか，それぞれ3つに分けて英語で示しなさい．

問2 2) intrinsically more powerful の主語は何か英語で示しなさい．

問3 3) Until the advent of methods that enabled genomewide surveys of association, researchers were therefore obliged to direct their attention to specific candidate variants or genes of interest. を日本語に訳しなさい．

問4 4) The number of loci for which there is convincing evidence that they confer susceptibility to type 2 diabetes started to grow in early 2007 with the publication of the first genomewide association studies. で述べている"the number"は現在いくつに増えているか数字で示しなさい．

問5 5) IRS1 (encoding insulin-receptor substrate 1) が他の遺伝子に比べてユニークな点は何か．日本語60字以内で答えなさい．

【問題 17】 次の英文を読んで，下の問に日本語で答えなさい．なお，解答に固有名詞が含まれる場合は本文のまま表記すること．

新潟大学　平成21年　919語　30〜35分

　　If the influence of the environment is partly prenatal, then the environment begins to sound a lot less like a malleable force and more like fate. Is this a peculiarity of ducks and geese, or are people also imprinted by the early environment with certain unvarying characteristics? Start with the medical clues. In 1989, a medical scientist named David Barker analyzed the fate of more than 5,600 men born between 1911 and 1930 in six districts of Hertfordshire in southern England. Those who had weighed the least at birth and at one year old went on to have the highest death rates from ischemic heart disease. The risk of death was nearly three times as great in the light babies as in the heavy babies.

　　a)Barker's result attracted much attention. It was no surprise that heavier babies should be more healthy, but it was a great surprise that they should be less vulnerable to a disease of old age, and one, moreover, for which the causes were supposedly well known. Here was evidence that heart disease is influenced less by how much cream you eat as an adult than by how thin you were at one year old. Barker has gone on to confirm the same result in data from other parts of the world for heart disease, stroke, and diabetes. For instance, among 4,600 men born in Helsinki University Hospital between 1934 and 1944, those who were thin or light at birth and at one year old were far more likely to die of coronary heart disease. Barker puts it this way: b)had none of these people been thin as babies, then there would have been half as much coronary heart disease later — a huge potential gain in public health.

　　Barker argues that heart disease cannot be understood as an accumulation of environmental effects during life. "Rather, the consequences of some influences, including a high body mass in childhood, depend on events at early critical stages of development. This embodies the concept of developmental 'switches' triggered by the environment." According to the "thrifty phenotype" hypothesis, which has grown out of this work, Barker has found an adaptation to famine. The body of a poorly nourished baby, imprinted with prenatal experience, is born "expecting" a state of food deprivation throughout life. The baby's metabolism is geared to being small, hoarding calories, and avoiding excessive exercise. When, instead, the baby finds itself in a time of plenty, it compensates by growing fast but in such a way as to put a strain on its heart.

c) The famine hypothesis may have even more bizarre implications, as revealed by an "accidental experiment" conducted on a vast scale during the Second World War. It began in September 1944, at a time when the former collaborators Konrad Lorenz and Niko Tinbergen were both in captivity. Lorenz was in a Russian prisoner-of-war camp, having just been captured; Tinbergen was about to be released after two years in a German internment camp where he was held hostage under threat of death against the activities of the Dutch resistance. On 17 September 1944, British paratroopers occupied the Dutch city of Arnhem to capture a strategic bridge over the Rhine. Eight days later, the Germans forced them to surrender, having fought off the ground forces sent to their relief. The Allies then abandoned attempts to liberate Holland until after the winter.

The Dutch railway workers had called a strike to try to prevent German reinforcements from reaching Arnhem. In retaliation, Reichskommissar Arthur Seyss-Inquart ordered an embargo on all civilian transport in the country. The result was a devastating famine, which lasted for seven months: the hunger winter, they called it. More than 10,000 people starved to death. But what later caught the attention of medical researchers was d) the effect that this abrupt famine had on unborn babies. Some 40,000 people were foetuses during the famine, and their birthweight and later health are all on record. In the 1960s a team from Columbia University studied the data. They found all the expected effects of malnourished mothers: malformed babies, high infant mortality, and high rates of stillbirth. But they also found that those babies who were in their last trimester of gestation suffered from low birth weight. These babies grew up normal, but they later suffered from diabetes, probably brought on by the mismatch between their thrifty phenotype and the abundant rich food of the post-war world.

Babies who were in the first six months of gestation during the famine were normal in birth weight, but when they reached adulthood they themselves gave birth to unusually small babies. This bizarre second generation effect is hard to explain with the thrifty phenotype hypothesis, though Pat Bateson notes that locusts take several generations to switch from a shy, solitary form with a specialist diet to the swarming, gregarious form with a generalist diet and back again. If it takes several generations for humans to switch between thrifty and affluent phenotypes, this may explain why e) Finland has nearly four times the death rate from heart disease as in France. The government of France began supplementing the rations of pregnant mothers after the Franco-Prussian war of the 1870s. The people of Finland lived in comparative poverty until 50 years ago. Perhaps it is the first two generations to experience abundance who suffer from heart disease. Perhaps that is why the United States is now seeing rapidly falling death rates from heart disease, but Britain, well fed for a shorter time, is lagging behind.

（出典：Matt Ridley, *NATURE VIA NURTURE - Genes, Experience, and What Makes Us Human*, HarperCollins, 2003）

《語注》
ischaemic heart disease：虚血性心疾患　　coronary heart disease：冠動脈性心疾患
trimester：全妊娠期間の1/3にあたる3ヶ月　　Reichskommissar：占領地弁務官
Arthur Seyss-Inquart：アルトゥル＝インクヴァルト（1892－1946，ナチスドイツの高官）

問1　a)の内容を本文に即して説明しなさい．

問2　b)を和訳しなさい．

問3　c)の内容を本文に即して説明しなさい．

問4　d)の内容を本文に即して説明しなさい．

問5　e)の理由を本文に即して説明しなさい．

【問題 18】 次の英文を読んで以下の設問に答えなさい．
高知大学　平成21年　1642語　40分

Alzheimer's Disease

My mom, who is in a nursing home, developed Alzheimer's disease at age 74. How high is my risk?

Over the last century, as the average human life span has dramatically increased, declining mental function in old age has become an immense medical and societal problem. From 1907 when Dr. Alois Alzheimer described the autopsy study of the brain of a woman for whom he had cared over several years, until about 1960, there was relatively little attention paid to dementia in the elderly. In just 40 years, Alzheimer's disease (AD), once considered as a relatively unimportant consequence of aging, has emerged as the most serious medical problem among older patients.

The major feature of AD is a gradual (and, eventually, dramatic) loss of memory, especially for recent events. Over time, speech also declines and vocabulary shrinks. The individual tends to repeat questions asked of him or her, loses the ability to follow simple directions, and becomes easily lost in all but the best-known surroundings. Even the personality changes; the patient loses social skills and may become paranoid. Eventually, he or she has trouble walking. A person suffering from AD inhabits a world that grows smaller each day. In the end, patients are bedridden and require total care. They often die of pneumonia.

Especially in the early stages of the disease, the diagnosis is difficult to make with certainty. There is no blood test or X-ray study with which to confirm the clinical suspicion. Even today, AD is a diagnosis of exclusion, meaning that the physician will make it only after he has excluded all other possible causes. An experienced diagnostician will correctly diagnose the disease more than 90% of the time, but only a postmortem study of the brain provides absolute proof.

AD is uncommon before the age of 60 and is diagnosed in only about 1% of persons who are 65. On the other hand, AD is relatively common among people over the age of 75, and its incidence rises steadily with age. Some studies indicate that almost one-half of those over the age of 85 have signs and symptoms compatible with AD. Although there are many causes of dementia, most are thought to be due to AD. Estimates of the number of affected Americans now hover around the 4,000,000 mark. The disease seems as common in one nation as another. Many neurologists believe that the longer one lives, the more likely he or she will develop AD.

No one knows what causes AD. Over the years, many credible theories have been proposed, but none has been proven and many have been refuted. For example, at one time some scientists believed that the disease arose due to a toxic accumulation of trace amounts of aluminum. Today, the dominant theory is that AD is caused by an unusual precipitation of a brain protein called β-amyloid, but an important minority of researchers in the field continue to explore other possibilities. One, Dr. John Nash of Massachusetts General Hospital, has begun to convince people that excess copper and zinc may play an important role. He believes that the amyloid protein acts as a sponge to soak up the heavy metals which are the true culprits. A small clinical trial in which patients with AD were treated with a drug that acts to limit accumulation of these metals showed that it slows disease progression.

Physicians have long known that AD sometimes runs in families and that there are a few families in which many people develop a severe form of the disorder in their 40s or 50s. Armed with the new tools of DNA analysis, during the late 1980s and 1990s, scientists made a series of exciting discoveries concerning the role of genes in AD. Today we know of several genes, which, when mutated, confer grave risk for a very early onset form of the disease. In addition, scientists have found other regions of the human genome that appear to include genes which predispose to the far more common late-onset form of AD.

The first report of a predisposing gene for early-onset AD grew out of the observation that essentially all persons born with Down syndrome (which is caused by the presence of an extra chromosome 21) develop AD if they live into their 50s.

Amyloid, the protein that is found in excess in the brains of persons with AD, is coded for by a gene on chromosome 21 called APP (amyloid precursor protein). Examining rare families with early-onset AD, scientists eventually found a handful of cases worldwide where the disease was clearly caused by mutations in APP.

Studying other highly unusual families, other researchers were able to find mutations in genes on chromosomes 1 and 14 that explained their early-onset disease. The gene on chromosome 14 is called the PS1 (presenilin 1) gene and that on chromosome 1 is called the PS2 gene. PS1 accounts for about half of the early-onset cases, and more than 50 different "familial" mutations have been found. Mutations in PS2 explain the early onset of AD in a cluster of families of Volga-German background. The discovery of mutations that explain only a tiny fraction of all cases still greatly helps in the effort to understand how the disease arises. Of course, the real goal is to untangle the genetic contribution to the late-onset form of AD that burdens tens of millions of people around the world. At the center of that effort is a gene called APOE on chromosome 19.

In 1991, a study showed that in families with more than one person with AD, affected individuals were more likely to have the same version of a certain part of chromosome 19 than would be expected by chance. By l993, a team at Duke University showed that the gene in question was APOE, already well studied because it coded for a cholesterol transport protein. Large family studies soon showed that of the three common forms of the gene (E2, E3, and E4, which are found on 7%, 78%, and 15% of chromosomes among Caucasians), E4 was associated with risk for AD.

The most important discovery was that the 2-3% (a number arrived at by multiplying 15% by 15% because the chance of inheriting a copy from one parent is independent of the chance of inheriting a copy from another parent) of persons born with two copies of APOE4 were far more likely to have AD than were age-matched controls who did not have two copies. Other studies showed that E2 seemed to protect against AD. Persons with two copies of E2 were less likely to have the disease, and if they did have it, were more likely to develop symptoms at an older age.

Although APOE status is currently the most important known risk factor for AD, it alone is not predictive enough to constitute a screening test. This is because many people who develop AD do not have an E4 allele, and many who do not develop AD do carry an E4 allele. Current estimates are that APOE status explains about 50% of the genetic effect on risk for late-onset disease. This raises the possibility that the discovery of one or two other relatively common genetic factors could lead to the creation of a fairly accurate risk test. Preliminary research by workers at the University of Arkansas suggests that common variants of a gene called IL-1 (which codes for a protein that plays a central role in the body's inflammatory response) may be another important risk factor.

In 2002, the National Institute on Aging launched the most ambitious effort yet to track down other genes that predispose to AD. Under the coordination of neurologist Richard Mayeux at Columbia University, researchers are recruiting 1000 families in which AD is common. Given the vast number of subjects and our ever more impressive gene-finding tools, it is likely that they will discover several new predisposing genes.

Should people with a family history of late-onset AD be tested for APOE4?

Most physicians discourage such inquiries. However, there are some situations in which testing is valuable. It is most helpful in clinical situations in which a physician strongly suspects the diagnosis. If the patient has two copies of E4, that finding strongly supports the suspicion. Another context in which testing for APOE status may be helpful is if an affected parent is known to carry two copies of the E4 allele. It may be reassuring to the children to find that they carry only one copy.

　To confront the question with which I opened this section, having a parent who developed AD after age 70 is so common, and the etiology is so complex, that one can say little more than that it probably suggests a somewhat greater risk to the children than if were（筆者注：「there」の間違いであろう）was no family history. Currently, APOE4 testing would be of little benefit to those children. However, the risk for, and age at onset of, AD are both definitely influenced by genetic factors. It is likely that a risk assessment test with reasonable predictive value could appear in the next 5 years. Since the disease is incurable, if such a test is developed, it will be engulfed in ethical debate. Likely, the choice to use it will be driven less by clinical than by life-planning considerations.

Table, Alzheimer's disease: Familial risk
Three dominant genes cause three extremely rare forms of AD with early age of onset.
APOE4 allele accounts for about 55% of the overall risk for the common form of AD.
In persons born with two copies of the APOE4 allele (about 3% of northern Europeans) who do develop AD, the age of onset is more than a decade earlier than among those affected persons who do not have these alleles.
APOE4 testing is not a good predictor of risk. Many people with these alleles do not develop the disease.

(出典：Philip Reilly, *Is It in Your Genes? The Influence of Genes on Common Disorders and Diseases That Affect You and Your Family,* CSHL Press, 2004)

問1　a～dのうち，アルツハイマー病について本文の内容と合致するものを選びなさい．

a. 肺炎で死ぬことが多い．
b. 発症後すぐから，記憶が急激に衰える．
c. 迷子になりやすい．
d. 偏執的になることがある．

1. a	2. b	3. c	4. d
5. a, b	6. a, c	7. a, d	8. b, c
9. b, d	10. c, d	11. a, b, c	12. a, b, d
13. a, c, d	14. b, c, d	15. a, b, c, d	16. すべて誤り

問2　a～dのうち，アルツハイマー病の診断および原因について，本文の内容と合致するものを選びなさい．

a. 脳のX線写真で診断できる．
b. 85歳以上の半数がアルツハイマー病の兆候・症状を持つ．
c. アルミニウムの脳への蓄積が原因である．
d. 過剰の銅・亜鉛が重要な役割を果たしている可能性は否定された．

1. a	2. b	3. c	4. d
5. a, b	6. a, c	7. a, d	8. b, c
9. b, d	10. c, d	11. a, b, c	12. a, b, d
13. a, c, d	14. b, c, d	15. a, b, c, d	16. すべて誤り

問3　a～dのうち，アルツハイマー病の原因遺伝子について，本文の内容と合致するものを選びなさい．

a. 第21番染色体を余分にもつことで発症するダウン症候群の患者は，50歳を超えるとそのほとんどがアルツハイマー病になる．
b. 第1番染色体にあるアミロイド前駆体タンパク質遺伝子が変異してアルツハイマー病を発症することがある．
c. 40～50歳代でアルツハイマー病を発症する人たちは遺伝子の変異が原因である可能性が高い．
d. ボルガ-ゲルマンの遺伝的背景を持つ人々は，1番染色体上のプレセニリン2に異常

があることでアルツハイマー病を早期に発症することがある．

1. a	2. b	3. c	4. d
5. a, b	6. a, c	7. a, d	8. b, c
9. b, d	10. c, d	11. a, b, c	12. a, b, d
13. a, c, d	14. b, c, d	15. a, b, c, d	16. すべて誤り

問4　a～dのうち，APOEについて本文の内容と合致するものを選びなさい．

a. APOEはコレステロールを輸送するタンパク質をコードしている．
b. 第19番染色体上にある．
c. APOEには，E2, E3, E4が知られる．
d. APOEのE4タイプをもつヒトは40～50歳代でアルツハイマー病を発症する場合が多い．

1. a	2. b	3. c	4. d
5. a, b	6. a, c	7. a, d	8. b, c
9. b, d	10. c, d	11. a, b, c	12. a, b, d
13. a, c, d	14. b, c, d	15. a, b, c, d	16. すべて誤り

問5　a～dのうち，APOEとアルツハイマー病について，本文の内容と合致するものを選びなさい．

a. コーカシアンのうち，2～3％がAPOE4を2コピーもち，2コピーもたないヒトよりもアルツハイマー病を発症しやすい．
b. APOE2はアルツハイマー病を予防している．
c. APOE2を2コピーもつヒトはアルツハイマー病になりにくいか，もたない人より発症が遅いと考えられている．
d. APOE4遺伝子は，コーカシアンの第19番染色体の15％に見つかる．

1. a	2. b	3. c	4. d
5. a, b	6. a, c	7. a, d	8. b, c
9. b, d	10. c, d	11. a, b, c	12. a, b, d
13. a, c, d	14. b, c, d	15. a, b, c, d	16. すべて誤り

問6　a～dのうち，APOEとアルツハイマー病について，本文の内容と合致するものを選びなさい．

a. APOEだけではアルツハイマー病のリスクを予見することはできない．
b. APOE4をもつヒトでもアルツハイマー病を発症しない場合がある．
c. APOE4をもたないヒトでもアルツハイマー病を発症する場合がある．
d. 40～50歳代でアルツハイマー病を発症する場合の50％は，APOE4で説明できる．

1. a	2. b	3. c	4. d
5. a, b	6. a, c	7. a, d	8. b, c
9. b, d	10. c, d	11. a, b, c	12. a, b, d
13. a, c, d	14. b, c, d	15. a, b, c, d	16. すべて誤り

問7　a～dのうち，遺伝子診断とアルツハイマー病について，本文の内容と合致するものを選びなさい．

a. アルツハイマー病の患者を家系内にもつヒトはAPOE4の遺伝子を調べるべきである．
b. アルツハイマー病の治療法が確立していないのにAPOE4などの遺伝子診断を行うことには，倫理的な問題がある．
c. 最初の質問，「*My mom, who is in a nursing home, developed Alzheimer's disease at age 74. How high is my risk?*」には，家族にアルツハイマー病のヒトがいない場合よりは確実に高いと答える．
d. 炎症には中心的な役割を果たすIL-1をコードする遺伝子の変異は新たな遺伝的要因である可能性がある．

1. a	2. b	3. c	4. d
5. a, b	6. a, c	7. a, d	8. b, c
9. b, d	10. c, d	11. a, b, c	12. a, b, d
13. a, c, d	14. b, c, d	15. a, b, c, d	16. すべて誤り

【問題19】以下の英文を読んで設問に答えなさい．
鹿児島大学　平成15年　765語　45分

As scientists race to unravel the mysteries of SARS, one issue high on their agenda will be the likelihood that the new virus is a cross-species transmission in which the virus has mutated from its animal carrier so that it can infect humans, who have no immunity from the alien invader. The most obvious examples of this are HIV and influenza, and the latter disease has disturbing parallels with SARS. The flu virus lives usually in the stomachs of waterfowl, and the two are co-adapted — the birds don't get sick. It is widely believed among virologists, however, that with the domestication of ducks in southern China 2,000-3,000 years ago, flu jumped species. This region has always had high densities of people living in close proximity to large populations of pigs and chickens. It's not known in which order, but with this ready pool of targets near at hand, flu has transferred from ducks to all three species—and once established, it can swap back and forth between its different new hosts with devastating effect.

（中　略）

In 1997, Hong Kong's "bird flu" was a virus that was part human, part avian. Much luck, hard scientific labor and prompt containment measures prevented that outbreak from turning into a global catastrophe. Next time we might not be so fortunate. Medical records dating back to the 18th century show waves of influenza rolling westward from Asia through Russia into Europe with disturbing regularity. Three or four times a century, a pandemic spreads from flu's heartland. So statistically speaking, since the last reassorted strain emerged in Hong Kong in 1968, we're due for another one.

Every pandemic is calamitous. The "Russian flu" of 1889-90 is thought to have killed 250,000 people in Europe alone. No epidemic, however — not even the Black Death of the Middle Ages— compares in mortality to the "Spanish flu" of 1918. Around the world, 40 million died of it within one year. Unusually, the 1918 flu did not come from Asia. The first outbreak began at a barracks in Kansas in the spring. The second, most virulent strain of the disease emerged simultaneously in September in Boston, Massachusetts; in Brest on the Atlantic coast of France; and in Freetown, the capital of Sierra Leone.

The unusual origin, spread and potency of the 1918 flu are almost certainly connected to World War I, which saw large numbers of men crowded together in camps, transports and trenches. We don't know exactly why this particular strain was more deadly than others—though scientists may be closing in on the answer — but we do know that it caused a global disaster. In Philadelphia, 7,500 people died of it in two weeks. The supply of coffins ran out; streetcars were used as hearses. Families lay dying in their homes, unable even to stir to feed themselves. Some lingered in delirium for weeks, coughing foamy, blood-tinged sputum, while others were dead within 24 hours.

We cannot be sure whether the next pandemic will be this bad, any more than we can be sure when it will come or where it will start. ① There is only one thing of which we can be certain: that it definitely will happen again. We can also be sure that, as so often before, it very likely may begin in southern China. Variants of the strain that caused the "bird-flu" outbreak six years ago are still cropping up around the region, or the outbreak could arise from some other strain altogether.

Professor Kennedy Shortridge of the University of Hong Kong has run blood tests on birds, animals and people in the territory, in Taiwan, in Jiangsu province and in the Pearl River Delta. Especially in the latter two places, he found farmers with antibodies suggesting exposure to every single type of flu that exists in other species. So it's just a matter of time before one of those types adapts to human beings and takes off.

In the meantime, we wait to see if SARS can adapt with the same deadly efficiency as influenza — and once a virus achieves airborne transmission from one person to another, the consequences might be as brutal as the 1918 flu that killed one in 60 of all the people on earth. Perhaps if we knew that SARS had come from another species, we could identify how it had changed and we could design drugs or vaccines to tackle it. By the time we had produced them, however, the disease would already have done its deadly damage. Once again, we find ourselves ② at the mercy of nature.

(出典：Pete Davies, "*The Cycle of Death*" Time, 2003)

《語注》
unravel：解明する
agenda：協議事項
waterfowl：水鳥
flu：インフルエンザ
devastating：破壊的な
containment：封じ込め
pandemic：世界的流行の

SARS：重症急性呼吸器症候群
animal carrier：保有動物
virologist：ウイルス学者
host：宿主
avian：鳥類の
catastrophe：大惨事

reassorted strain：遺伝子再集合ウイルス株（インフルエンザウイルスは8本のRNA鎖をもち，組み合わせの違うウイルスが同時に感染すると遺伝子の混ぜ合わせが起こり新しいウイルス株が出現する）
calamitous：悲惨な　　　　　　　　　epidemic：流行
virulent：毒性の強い　　　　　　　　potency：影響力
trench：塹壕　　　　　　　　　　　　coffin：棺桶
hearse：霊柩車　　　　　　　　　　　delirium：せん妄（一時的精神錯乱状態）
blood-tinged sputum：血痰　　　　　Jiangsu province：江蘇州
antibody：抗体　　　　　　　　　　　airborne：空気によって運ばれる

問1　1997年の香港型インフルエンザの流行では，なぜ危機的な大流行が防がれたのでしょう．その理由を日本語で解答欄に書きなさい．

問2　1918年のスペイン型インフルエンザが広範囲に流行したのはなぜですか．その理由を日本語で解答欄に書きなさい．

問3　下線部①において筆者がこのように確信する根拠はどのようなことですか．日本語で解答欄に書きなさい．

問4　下線部②は，具体的にどのようなことを示すのか．300字以内にまとめ，日本語で解答欄に横書きで書きなさい．

解答・解説

問題を解く前に
　和訳問題を解く際には，英文法のルールに従って，正確に文の構造をつかみ，1文1文を直訳できるようにしてほしい．直訳のままでは，不自然な日本語になることが多いので，文脈や常識等を考慮して，できるだけ自然な日本語に意訳することも必要となる．また，未知の単語が出てきた場合には，できるだけ前後関係から意味を推測するように心懸けること．以下の「訳し方のコツ」で，意訳する際に知っておくとよいテクニックを紹介しておく．

★訳し方のコツ
§1　無生物主語構文の訳し方
①英文の主語を「時，場所，手段，原因，理由」などを表す副詞として訳す．
②英文の目的語を主語にする．
③英文の動詞を，②に合わせて適切に訳し変える → 動詞を受動態化したり，自動詞化する場合が多い．

例文：The feeling of being neglected breeds our dissatisfaction.
〔和訳1〕無視されているという感覚が，私たちの不満を生む．
　→直訳である．この直訳でも自然な日本語になっているので，十分な答案となる．直訳が自然な日本語になるなら，それを答案とするのが一番よい．
〔和訳2〕無視されているという感覚①から，②不満が③生じる．
　→上記①〜③を使って意訳している．
〔補足〕和訳2では，「our」という代名詞を訳していない．代名詞は無視して訳してもよい場合がある．

§2　文の途中で切って訳すという発想
例文1：The sun provides us with light and heat.
〔和訳1〕太陽は私たちに光と熱を与えてくれる．
〔和訳2〕太陽が私たちに与えてくれるものがある．それは，光と熱だ．
　→ここでは，和訳1の直訳で十分である．しかし，和訳2のような訳し方もできるこ

とを頭にいれておいてほしい.「The sun provides us」までをいったん訳し，その後,「with light and heat」の訳をつけ足すのである.

例文2：It is important to get moderate exercise.
〔和訳1〕適度な運動を行うことは，重要である.
〔和訳2〕重要なことがある．それは，適度な運動を行うことだ.

例文3：This technology enabled us to develop a cure for Alzheimer's disease.
〔和訳1〕この技術により，私たちは，アルツハイマー病の治療法を開発できた.
〔和訳2〕この技術により，私たちができるようになったことがある．それは，アルツハイマー病の治療法の開発である.
→「V O to do」という形で to do 以下が長いときには，「文の途中で切って訳すという発想」が役に立つ可能性が高くなる.

§3 関係代名詞の訳し方
1 継続用法の訳し方
　適当な接続詞を補うと同時に，関係代名詞も普通の代名詞になおして訳せることがある.
例文1：Keiko has a daughter, who is a famous singer.
例文2：Many people discriminated against Hideo, whose father was a killer.（= for his father was a killer.）
例文3：The doctor gave me some antibiotics, which had no effect on me.（= but they had no effect on me.）
例文4：Medical science never interested Mike, whose father was a doctor.（= though his father was a doctor.）
例文5：I was a little surprised at the question, which seemed to have nothing to do with the subject of our conversation.（= for it seemed to have nothing to do with the subject of our conversation.）

2　1と同じ方法を限定用法にも使うことができる場合がある.
例文1：The woman whom I thought to be a scholar turned out to be a swindler.
〔和訳1〕私が学者だと思っていた女性が，詐欺師だとわかった.
〔和訳2〕その女性を学者だと私は思っていたけれども，詐欺師であることが判明した.
　→ここでは，和訳1（普通の訳し方）で十分であり，わざわざ和訳2の訳し方を採用する必要はない．ただし，こういう訳し方もできるということを知っておいてほしい.

例文2：The doctor performed a medical test which I thought was unnecessary.
〔和訳1〕その医師は，私が必要ないと思っていた医学的検査を行った.

〔和訳2〕その医師は，ある医学的検査を行った．しかし，私は，その検査は不必要であると思っていた．
　→英文の下線部を，「but I thought it was unnecessary」くらいに読みかえている．このように読みかえると，語順通りの訳が可能になる点に注目してほしい．関係代名詞節を訳すときは，節を訳してから先行詞にもどるという形が一般的であるが，このように，語順通り訳したほうが自然な日本語になることもある．

例文3：It is because of evolution that living things have grown into the profusion and diversity which make our planet very wonderful.
〔和訳〕進化が起こったからこそ，生物は豊富で多様になったのだ．この豊富さや多様性のおかげで，私たちの惑星はとてもすばらしい惑星となっているのだ．
　→下線部を，「and these make our planet very wonderful.」と読みかえている．

3　「前置詞＋関係代名詞」の先行詞が，「程度」「割合」「様態」を表す名詞の場合には，疑問詞節的な訳にするとよい場合がある．
例文1：We must determine the extent to which a patient's medical records should be disclosed for proper treatment.
〔和訳〕私たちは，適切な治療を行うために，患者のカルテがどの程度まで開示されるべきかを決めなければいけない．

例文2：Do you know the rate at which they divided the profit?
〔和訳〕彼らがどんな割合で利益を分配したか知っていますか．

例文3：How long a car lasts depends on the care with which it is used.
〔和訳〕車がどれだけ長持ちするかは，どれだけ気をつけてその車が使われるかにかかっている．

§4　受動態の訳し方
　能動態を意識して訳したほうがすっきりとした日本語になることが多い．
例文1：The part of speech of a word is determined by how it is used in the sentence.
〔和訳1〕ある言葉の品詞は，文章中でそれがどのように使われるかによって決められる．
〔和訳2〕ある言葉の品詞は，文章中での使い方によって決まる．
　→〔和訳1〕でもよいが，〔和訳2〕のようにもできる．

例文2：At the station we were met by two university students.
〔和訳1〕駅で，私たちは2人の大学生に出迎えられた．
〔和訳2〕駅で，2人の大学生が私たちを出迎えてくれた．

→〔和訳2〕は，能動態になおして訳している．by がついているときは，このような発想で訳せる．

§5 名詞の文章化
1 「名詞A of 名詞B」という形の of について
「of を含む名詞句の文章化」ができると訳の幅が広がる．
①所有格
　例：the dog of Mike
　→「マイクがその犬を持っている」という文章をイメージして「マイクが飼っている犬」という訳も可能．
②主格＝Aを動詞化すると，Bはその主語に当たるという関係がある場合
　例：the appearance of SARS
　→ SARS appears という文章をイメージできれば，訳の幅が広がる．
　例：The appearance of SARS made us uneasy.
　（SARS が出現したことで，私たちは不安になった．）
③目的格＝Aを動詞化すると，Bはその目的語に当たるという関係がある場合
　例：the discovery of antibiotics
　→ discover antibiotics（抗生物質を発見する）というイメージをもてるようにすること．
〔参考〕②③の場合には，名詞Aの部分の単語を見ると，すぐにその動詞形が頭に浮かぶであろう．appearance であれば appear, discovery であれば discover である．こういう場合には，この動詞形をイメージして訳を考えると訳の幅が広がる．
④同格＝AとBが同格の関係にある場合．
　例：the name of John ＝ジョンという名前
　例：There is little hope of his getting better.
　（彼が回復するという見込みはほとんどない）

　例文1：Nothing is so important as the proper choice of books to read.
　〔和訳1〕読むべき本の適切な選択ほど重要なことはない．
　〔和訳2〕読むべき本を適切に選択することほど重要なことはない．
　→和訳1で十分だが，和訳2も参考にしてほしい．和訳2では，「the proper choice of books to read ＝ properly choosing books to read」と捉えている．

　例文2：When they need something, babies cry. Your knowledge of this basic fact allows you to assume that a baby who is not crying needs nothing.
　〔和訳1〕何かが必要な時には，赤ん坊は泣く．この基本的な事実についての知識が，あなたに，泣いていない赤ん坊は何も必要としていないと推定することを可能にする．
　〔和訳2〕何かが必要な時には，赤ん坊は泣く．この基本的な事実を知っていれば，あ

なたは，泣いていない赤ん坊は何も必要としていないと推定することができる．
〔和訳3〕何かが必要な時には，赤ん坊は泣く．この基本的な事実を知っていれば，推定できることがある．それは，泣いていない赤ん坊は何も必要としていないということだ．
→〔和訳1〕よりも，〔和訳2〕のほうがわかりやすい日本語になっているのは明らかである．「Your knowledge of this basic fact ＝ you know this basic fact」と捉えている．下線部は無生物主語構文なので，§1で学んだことも使うこと．また，〔和訳3〕は，§2で学んだことを使っている．

2 所有格の訳し方：主語を表す所有格，目的語を表す所有格を見抜く
　所有格には，後ろの名詞を所有している主体を表す用法のほかに，次の用法がある．それは，後ろの名詞を動詞化したときに，その主語や目的語になっている用法である．このような関係を意識しておくとうまく訳せる場合がある（ただし，直訳でもそれほど不自然な訳にはならないことが多いとは思う）．
例文1（主格）：After their arrival, I called them. ＝ After they arrived, I called him.
例文2（目的格）：He was not her admirer. ＝ He was not a person who admired her.

§6 逆転の法則（とてもよく使う）

　「形容詞（的な働きをする語）＋名詞」という形は，「名詞」「形容詞」の順番で訳すとよい場合が度々ある．次の文の下線部の訳し方に注目してほしい．
Stewart *et al.* (2000) showed that the degree of patient-centred communication was associated with less discomfort, less concern and better mental health in patients.
〔和訳〕患者本位のコミュニケーションがどの程度行われているかが患者の不快感の軽減，不安の軽減，精神衛生の向上に関係してくるということをスチュアートらは示した．

第1章
設問形式別問題演習

1.1 和訳問題・内容説明問題

p.1【問題1】 愛媛大学 平成14年

問題の特徴

医学部学士編入試験（以下では学士試験と記す）を突破するうえで必要な基本的素養が試される問題と思われる．標準的な下線部和訳問題と内容説明問題から構成されており，30分という目標時間もちょうどよいくらいである．ただし，語数は短い．このような語数が短い英文ばかりが出題されるわけではないので，その点は勘違いしないでほしい．

解答

問1　下線（1）【解答例】 肥満にならないように絶えず努力していても肥満になる人もいる一方で，意識して（体重）管理を行っていなくても痩せたままの人もいる．

【解説】

下線（1）：① Some become obese despite a continuous struggle ② not to, whereas ③ others stay lean without conscious control.

①③ some と others の対応表現に注意．「…する人（物）もいれば，～する人（物）もいる」というイメージで捉えること．

例文：Some people like cats, and others like dogs.（猫好きな人もいれば，犬好きの人もいる）

②「not to ＝ not to become obese」であることに気づくこと．「become obese」のくり返しを避けている．

下線（3）【解答例】 この体の自動制御システムの構成要素を特定できれば，私たちが肥満になりやすいかどうかを決めている遺伝的かつ代謝的な素因を理解するのに役立つだろう．そして，肥満を防ぐためのよりよい治療法の開発にも役立つであろう．

【解説】

下線（3）：① Identifying components of the body's autoregulatory system that induce DIT will ② help us to understand the genetic and metabolic basis of susceptibility to obesity, and to develop better anti-obesity therapies.

①動名詞 identifying が主語を形成している．
② help O（to）do … ＝ O が…するのを助ける，O が…するのに役立つ
＊この下線部では，to do に該当する部分が 2 つある点（to understand と to develop）に注意．

　この問題は，意訳して自然な日本語にしないと高得点は望めない．なぜならば，①をふまえて直訳しただけでは，採点官が読みやすい自然な答案にはならないからだ．下線（3）は主語が長く，help 以下も長い．また，「genetic and metabolic basis of susceptibility to obesity」という訳しづらそうな語句も入っている．直訳しただけではかなり不自然な日本語になり，大幅な減点対象となるであろう．このことは他の問題にも当然当てはまることだが，この問題の場合は特に注意してほしい．

〔語句〕susceptibility ＝感受性，影響を受けやすいこと，（病気等に）かかりやすいこと

下線（4）【解答例】 しかし，様々な組織の中での交感神経の活動は，過食状態の際に高まり，エネルギーを保存しなくてはいけない状態，すなわち，飢餓状態の際には低下するということをランズベルクらが証明した時にようやく，交感神経が食物と熱発生を関連づけている遠心性システムとして位置づけられるようになった．

【解説】

　下線（4）：But ① it was not until Landsberg *et al.* demonstrated that ② SNS activity in a variety of tissues is boosted during overfeeding and decreased during starvation（a state of energy conservation）③ that the SNS was cast as the efferent system linking diet and thermogenesis.

①③「It is not until ～ that … ＝～してはじめて…する」という構文が登場している．
　例文：It is not until you lose your health that you realize the value of it.（健康を失ってはじめてその価値がわかる）
　⇒まず，「not until you lose your health」を訳すと，「あなたが健康を失うまではずっとない」となる．では，何が「ずっとない」のかといえば，that 以下のこと（「健康の価値を悟ること」）である．このような直訳ができることが大切である．これを意訳すると，「～してはじめて…する」という訳になる．

②ここでは is boosted という受動態が登場している．直訳すると，「様々な組織の中での交感神経の活動は，過食状態の際に高められる」ということになる．しかし，「…過食状態の際に高まる」のほうが明らかに自然である．このように，「…される」という日本語に固執しないほうが自然に訳せる受動態がたくさん出てくるので，注意しておいてほしい．

〔語句〕be cast as … ＝…として位置づけられる

問2 【解答例】食物を直接熱に変換する過程．その規模は遺伝子や食事で決まる．（30字）

【解説】
　下線（2）の直前にある，「to convert food directly into heat」を訳せばよい．しかし，ここだけでは字数が足りないので，後ろの文（The magnitude of this apparent "energy wastage" is determined by the genetic makeup of the individual and by the composition of their diet.）を簡潔にまとめて解答に加えた．

問3 【解答例】3つのβアドレナリン受容体がすべて欠損しているマウスは，過食状態に置かれると熱産生を増加させることができず，かなりの肥満になってしまう．しかし，野生型のマウスは，熱産生を活性化させることで，過食状態でも肥満に抵抗することができる．（115字）

【解説】
・下線（5）以降の2つの文に，解答に必要な実験結果が書かれている．下線（5）以降に出てくる「β-adrenergic receptors」については，一応【2段落】の第1文で説明されている．しかし，「β-adrenergic receptors」が何か理解できていなくても，取りあえず解答はつくれるであろう．
・「in contrast to … ＝…とは対照的に」という表現が最終文に出てきている．この表現はしっかり理解しておく必要がある．
〔語句〕mediator ＝ メディエーター（a thing that influences something [and/or] makes it possible for it to happen）

p.3【問題2】 愛媛大学　平成16年

問題の特徴

学士試験に必要な基本的素養が試される問題である．英作文も出ているので総合的な英語力が問われる．ただし，英作文については，対策していなくても突破できる大学が多い．愛媛大学も，現在では，英作文の対策は不要な大学と見なしてよい（もちろん，いきなり出題される可能性はある）．

解答

問1　【解答例】 しかしながら，放射線量に関しては，それを下回れば，ガンになるいかなる危険性も存在しないという証明がなされている閾値は存在しないのだ．他方で，X線診断で使われているような放射線量ならば確実にガンを誘発するということを証明している信頼性のあるデータも存在しないのである．

【別解】 しかし，放射線量に関しては，次のような閾値は存在していない．その閾値とは，それを下回れば，ガンになるいかなる危険性も存在しないということが証明されている閾値のことだ．他方で，X線診断で使われているような放射線量ならば確実にガンを誘発するということを証明している信頼性のあるデータも存在しないのである．

【解説】

下線部分：However, there is no threshold of radiation dose ① <u>under which the absence of any cancer risk is proven</u>. On the other hand, there are no reliable data proving that ② <u>radiation doses as used in diagnostic X-rays do induce cancer</u>.

① 「前置詞＋関係代名詞」が節をつくっている．この節は，先行詞に説明を加えている．ここで出てきている which は，先行詞である「threshold of radiation dose（放射線量の閾値）」が「どれか」をこれから説明するよという合図である．「閾値」といってもいろいろあるので，「どれか」ということを明らかにするという感じである．そして，「どれか」を知りたければ，先行詞を which に代入して下線①を訳せばよい．訳すと，「その閾値の下では，ガンになるいかなる危険性も存在しないという証明がなされている」となる．これでどんな閾値なのかがわかる．後は，threshold の前に no があることに注意して訳出することになる．

② as used in diagnostic X-rays という部分がややわかりにくい．as が導く語群が，直前の名詞を修飾するという特殊な用法がある．次の2つの例文を見てほしい．

(1) Industry <u>as we know it</u> began in 1765.
　　（私たちが知っているような産業は 1765 年にはじまった）

(2) The sunrise <u>as (it was) seen from the top of the mountain</u> was a fine spectacle.
　　（この山の頂上から見える日の出は，絶景だ）＊it was は省略されることがある．
　　⇒下線②の as の後にも they are が省略されていると考えられる．

なお，as のこのような用法を知らなくても，文脈を頼りにして，常識的な訳出を行える能力も習得していかねばならない．

この問題を解くには，文法的能力と自然な日本語に意訳する能力の両方が必要．とくに，However ではじまる第1文を訳すと，ぎこちない和文になる人が多いと思われる．【解答例】と【別解】を参照して，訳出の仕方を検討してほしい．

〔語句〕threshold ＝敷居，はじめ，閾値

問 2 【解答例】被爆者はγ線のみならず，β線や，汚染された食べ物などを通じて，α線も浴びることになる．このような事態は，放射線検査を受けている患者には生じない一方で，被爆者の罹患率や死亡率の一因となるので問題だ．さらに，被爆者が浴びたγ線は，診断用X線のために使われるγ線とはエネルギースペクトルが異なっていた．（148字）

【解説】
1 「発癌リスクの推定に用いたデータの問題点」が書かれている箇所を見つけてきて和文に直す（当然だが，自分の頭で勝手に答えを考えてはいけない．答えに必要な箇所を英文中から見つけてくるという意識を徹底させてほしい）．
2 その和文を設問の条件に合うように修正する．まず「発癌リスクの推定に用いたデータ」とは何かがわからないと，解答に必要な箇所を見つけられない．【2段落】から，それが「原子爆弾被爆者のデータ」を指していることがわかる．この理解があれば，【3段落】の第1文中の「but the data have limitations.」が，「原子爆弾被爆者のデータには限界がある．」という意味であることがわかる．「限界がある」ということは，「問題点がある」ということになる．ここまでくれば，【3段落】の第2文以降に解答に必要な箇所が出てくることがわかる．

第2文： One limitation is that the survivors were not only directly exposed with γ rays from the bomb detonations but also with β radiation, and, most importantly, α radiation from contaminated food, water, and dust in the air.
第3文： This additional exposure will not occur in patients undergoing radiological examinations but contributes to the morbidity and mortality of the atomic bomb survivors.
第4文： Additionally the γ rays to which the atomic bomb survivors were exposed were of a different energy spectrum from that used for diagnostic X-ray.
第5文： Without better data, however, it is probably adequate to use the Japanese data.
第6文： But these additional concerns should be taken seriously and the derived numbers for the incidence of cancer caused by X-rays should be critically assessed in future investigations, because the cancer risk is probably over-

estimated with use of the Japanese data.

　第2文のOne limitationと第4文のAdditionally（さらに）に着眼すれば問題点が2つあることがわかる．第2文と第4文が解答に必要なのは自明であるが，第3文はどうか．第3文は，第2文で述べられたことが問題となる理由を説明している．単に「問題点を指摘しなさい」という設問で，制限字数ももっと短ければ，第3文は無視することになる．第3文は問題点そのものではないからだ．しかし本問では，「どのように指摘しているか」という指示なので，問題点そのものだけでなく，その理由を含めて説明しても，題意に反するとは見なされないであろう．また，制限字数を満たすためにも，第3文を解答に入れておくのがよい．

　ちなみに，ある箇所を解答に入れるべきかどうかが微妙な時はよく出てくる．時間があればじっくり考えればよいが，試験時間が短い学士試験ではそこまでの余裕がない場合も多い．そういう時には「大は小をかねる戦法」を使ってほしい．ようするに，迷った箇所はとりあえず答案に入れておくという戦法だ．それが余事記載（解答には必要のない記載）になっても，答案の他の箇所で重要なポイントをきちんと指摘できていれば，大きな減点は受けないであろう．

〔補足1〕第6文の下線部を見てほしい．これを読むと，ここも解答に入れるべきではないかと思う人もいるかもしれない．しかし，これは第2文や第4文で指摘された問題点を一言で言い換えたものと見ればよいであろう．あまりいろいろ考えすぎずに，第2文～第4文を機械的に訳して解答をサッとつくってしまうのがよいであろう．

〔補足2〕第4文の解答例の最後に「エネルギースペクトル」という物理用語が出てくる．語注や物理の知識がないと，この用語を使って解答を書くことは難しい．しかし，この訳語を使えなくてもまったくかまわない．重要なのは，100%正確でなくてもよいので，日本語を工夫して，常識的な内容の答案を書いておくことだ．この際，「spectrum＝範囲，領域」という知識があれば役立つ．

例1：被爆者が浴びたγ線と，診断用X線のために使われるγ線とでは，エネルギー領域（または範囲）が異なっていた．
→物理学的に正確な言い方かどうかは微妙だが，もっともらしい日本語には見える．
例2：被爆者が浴びたγ線は，診断用X線のために使われるγ線とは，エネルギー量が異なっていた．
例3：被爆者が浴びたγ線は，診断用X線のために使われるγ線と，エネルギーに関する点で異なっていた．
→例2，例3はspectrumの意味を知らない場合である．もちろん第4文の訳としては不正確であり，減点は受けるであろう．しかし，常識的にあり得ない内容ではない点に注目してほしい．単語がわからない時はこういう形で取り繕い，部分点を狙うことになる．

問3 【解答例】 X線診断には，癌の早期発見による早期治療という利益もあるが，発癌の危険性や在院日数が延びるというリスクもあるので，この利益とリスクを慎重に考慮して，無駄なX線検査はしないようにするべきである．（96字）

【解説】
1 【5段落】の最終文の「In everyday practice」に着眼する．これが設問文にある「日常診察」とほぼ合致すると考えられる．
2 【5段落】の最終文の「think carefully about the benefit for and the risk to their patients for each examination」が解答の中心となる．「benefitとriskを慎重に考慮する」というのが解答の骨格となる．しかしこれだけでは字数が足りないので，benefitとriskを具体化する．benefitについては【4段落】に書かれている．riskは【5段落】の第2文を見れば把握できる．

問4 【解答例】 ① There are two effects of radiation on the human body: a deterministic effect and a stochastic effect. ② A deterministic effect means that ③ exposure to radiation over a particular threshold always causes conditions such as radiation dermatitis or radiation cataracta. ④ A stochastic effect means that even exposure to a low-dose of radiation may increase a risk of having conditions such as anomaly or carcinogenesis.

【解説】
① 影響が2つあると述べてから，「：（コロン）」を使って，a deterministic effectとa stochastic effectを列挙している．その後は，②④のように順番に説明を加えている．
③ 「exposure to … ＝…への接触」という使い方は知っておくとよい．exposeという動詞を使いたければ，「being exposed to radiation」となる．主部なので動名詞化する必要がある．

【別解】 ① The effects of radiation on the human body are divided into two kinds: deterministic effects and stochastic effects. Deterministic effects result from being exposed to radiation over a particular threshold. Their examples include conditions such as radiation dermatitis or radiation cataracta. Stochastic effects result from exposure to a low-dose radiation. One of their examples is an increase in the risk of conditions such as anomaly or carcinogenesis.

【解説】
① divideを使って書いた．「classify（分類する）」を使ってもよい．ただし，〔解答例〕のような書き方で十分であり，あえてこれらの動詞を利用する必要はない．

p.5【問題3】 鹿児島大学　平成23年

問題の特徴

　鹿児島大学の英語の試験では，長文読解問題が2題出題される．下線部和訳の問題はほとんど出題されない．内容説明問題が主流である．本問も内容説明問題である．本問は下線部付きの内容説明問題だが，鹿児島大学では，下線部がない内容説明問題も数多く出題されている．下線部がある場合には，その周辺に解答に必要な箇所がある場合が多いので取り組みやすい．しかし下線部がない場合には，最初から全部目を通していかないと解答に必要な箇所が見つけづらいので注意．

　なお，鹿児島大学の英語の試験では，2題のうちどちらを先にやるかがとても重要になる．難しい問題からやってしまうと大変なことになる．試験開始と同時に問題をチェックし，簡単な問題から手をつけるようにしないといけない．

解答

問1　【解答例】子供に対するCT利用の増大をめぐるごたごたの中で，ブレナーは最も執拗な発言者になっているということ．彼は，多くの放射線医や医学物理学者とはまったく異なる主張をしている．それは，1回のCTのリスクは小さいが，毎年何十万人もの子供がCTを受けるとリスクが積み重なり，公衆衛生上の緊急問題になるというものだ．(150字)

【解説】

　下線部①を含む文の次の文，すなわち【2段落】の第3文をまず簡単にふまえたほうがよいであろう．「insistent（執拗な）」という単語がtroublemakerとなじむ．また【4段落】の最終文「With hundreds of thousands of children getting CT scans every year, that small individual risk balloons into a pressing public health concern, Brenner concluded.」と【5段落】の第1文，第2文を比較すると，ブレナーが多くの人の意見に反する主張をしていることがわかり，これがtroublemakerといわれる所以だということがわかる．

〔補足1〕解答をつくる際にふまえる箇所が，下線部から少し離れた所にもある点に注意．
〔補足2〕最後から5つ目の段落（By 2010ではじまる）にも実は，ブレナーの研究により迷惑を被った医師の話が出てきている．厳密にはこの段落もふまえて解答をつくるべきかもしれないが，下線部①を含む【2段落】からはだいぶ遠いので，微妙である．

問2　【解答例】1回のCTで浴びる放射線量と，1回分の放射線量で，致命的な癌が生じる確率を根拠にした．前者は1989年にイギリスで行われた成人のCT利用に関する調査結果を使って推定した．後者は広島と長崎の被曝者の発癌データを使って計算した．とくに，1回又は2回のCTで浴びるとされる5〜100ミリシーベルトの放射線を浴びた被爆

1.1　和訳問題・内容説明問題

者のデータを使った．さらに腹部と頭部へのCTが年に60万回行われたという事実も根拠とした．（200字）

【解説】
　下線部の直後の「he needed two pieces of information: the radiation delivered by a single CT scan, and the probability that a dose to a given organ would produce a fatal cancer there. For the first, he used a 1989 British survey of CT use in adults to estimate the dose children experience. For the second, Brenner turned to "the only quantitative tool we had and still have," he says: risk calculations of radiation-induced cancer in survivors of the atomic bombings of Hiroshima and Nagasaki.」が参考になる．さらに，【11段落】の最終文「Brenner based his risk…」も解答に入れられると具体的になってよい．また，【9段落】の第3文「But given that…」も入れられるとよい．

〔重要表現〕
given ～ ＝ ～を考慮に入れると（Nature等で頻出する表現である．「～」には名詞やthat節が入る）
例文1：Given the circumstances, you've done really well.
（その状況を考慮に入れると，あなたは本当に良くやった）
例文2：Given that the patients have some disabilities, we must support them so that they can be as independent as possible.
（その患者たちがいくつかの障害を抱えているということを考慮に入れると，私たちは彼らができるだけ自立できるように支援していかねばならない）

問3　【解答例】CTスキャンで使われる範囲内の放射線量に関する研究からは，意味のある生物学的な影響は一切明らかにならないという意見もある．なかには，放射線量が低量であれば，癌に対する保護作用が生じるということを示唆している研究もある．複数回CTスキャンを受けた患者でも，細胞には次のCTスキャンを受けるまでに自己を修復する能力があるから，損傷が蓄積するはずはなく，心配する必要はないという意見もある．原爆の生存者達に着眼することはおかしいという意見もある．（221字）

【解説】
　シンプルに，下線部の直後をまとめればよい．
〔語句〕　skeptical ＝ 懐疑的な　　　as for ～ ＝ ～に関する限り，～について言えば
　　　　cumulative ＝ 累積的な

p.10【問題4】新潟大学　平成19年

問題の特徴

　シンプルな下線部説明問題と下線部和訳問題である．学士試験における標準的な問題と思われる．とくに（3）の和訳問題はしっかりできてほしい．なお，新潟大学は，現在では試験科目から英語が消えた．その代わりにTOEICのスコア提出が義務づけられている．

解答

問1　【解答例】 妻が襲われた夜に負った頭部の怪我により，その夜以降，短期記憶を長期記憶に変換できなくなった男が，妻を殺した犯人を見つけて復讐しようとする話．彼は，捜査の過程でわかった手がかりを，体に入れ墨を入れて記録しなければならなかった．

【解説】
【1段落】を読めれば解答できる．

問2　【解答例】 ニューロンの核内の奥深くで生じた遺伝子の活性化が，どのようにして遠く離れたシナプスの働きを制御しているのかという問題．

【解説】
【5段落】の冒頭を参照．ニューロンの核内にある遺伝子がシナプスの連結に一役買っていることはわかっていたが（【4段落】の最終文），その遺伝子がどうやって遠くにあるシナプスを制御しているのかはわかっていなかった．【5段落】の第2文，第3文も解答に入れたいところだが，「簡潔に」という指示があるのでここでは解答に含めなかった．

問3【解答例】 タンパク質がつくられるためには，細胞の核内にあるひと続きのDNAが転写されて，mRNAという運搬可能な形態に変換されなければいけない．mRNAは，その後，細胞装置によりそれがもつ暗号化された指示がタンパク質に翻訳される場所に移動する．

【解説】
　下線部（c）：For a protein to be produced, a stretch of DNA inside the cell nucleus must be transcribed into a portable form called messenger RNA (mRNA), ① which then travels out to the place where cellular machinery translates its encoded instructions into a protein.

　下線部①は意訳して「mRNAは，その後特定の場所に移動する．そして，そこにある細胞装置により，mRNAがもつ暗号化された指示がタンパク質に翻訳される」としてもよいであろう．「where以下を訳して，直前のthe placeにかける」という訳し方を放棄

して，前から順に訳すという発想を採用している．このほうが自然な感じがする．

問4 【解答例】 その連結が一時的に強化されることで，このシナプスは，記憶を短期間だけ保持する能力を得た．それと同時に，シグナル伝達分子が出て，神経細胞の核にゆっくりと進んでいくのだ．核内に入ると，この伝達分子は，永続的にシナプスの連結を強化しようとするタンパク質を合成するために必要とされる適切な遺伝子を活性化しようとした．

【解説】

下線部 (d)：① With its connection temporarily strengthened, this synapse could hold the memory for a short time while the signaling molecule departed, wending its way to the nucleus of the nerve cell. There this messenger molecule would activate appropriate genes needed to synthesize proteins that would permanently strengthen the synaptic connection.

下線①では付帯状況の with が出てきている．with は「一緒に」というイメージなので，主節（ここでは，「this synapse could hold…」）と同時に起こっていることをつけ加えていると考えればよい．ここでは，「with ＋ 名詞 ＋ done」という形になっている点に注意．「名詞」と done の間に受動関係を読み取り，まずは「名詞が〜されるのと同時に」という感じで直訳するとよい．

〔語句〕wend one's way ＝ゆっくりと進む　　　synthesize ＝合成する

1.2　要約問題

p.13【問題5】東京工業大学大学院　平成20年

問題の特徴

　文の流れがはっきりと出ており，要約しやすい問題である．このような良問をたくさんこなすことが一番の対策になる．
　なお，○字程度と指定されている場合には，±10%の字数に収めること．

「要旨」と「要約」の違い

要旨 ＝ 筆者が一番述べたいこと（筆者の主張の中心部分）
要約 ＝「要旨」＋「要旨を述べるための道筋」（または，「元の文章の内容を，筆者の意図に沿って短くまとめたもの」という言い方でもよいだろう）
cf. 題名 ＝要旨を語句の形に縮めたもの（「題名をつけなさい」という問題も出てくる）

　「要約しなさい」という問題では，**各段落の要約をつくり，それらを最後につなげていくという発想が基本となる**．単につなげるだけでは駄目である．上記の要約の定義から考えれば，「筆者が展開している論理の道筋」がわかるようにつなげていくことになる．よって，筆者の主張との関連で重要度の低い段落の要約は削っていくという作業や，論理の道筋がわかりやすいように接続詞をうまく利用するなどの作業が必要となる．本問は要約問題なので，このような考え方で解くのが原則である．要約の答案を作成する際には，具体例や体験談や引用文や比喩などの記述はできるだけカットし，まとめ的な役割をはたしている抽象的な記述を拾っていくとよいであろう．
　「要旨を述べなさい」という問題では，上記の定義では，「筆者が一番述べたいこと」を書けばよいということになるが，字数に余裕があれば理由も簡潔な形で入れたほうがよい．
〔参考〕「要約しなさい」という問題は，上記の定義によれば，文全体の論理の道筋を理解しないと解答できないということになる．しかし，実際の試験の時には，論理の道筋を完全に確認できなくても，筆者が一番述べたいことと，その理由は何とかわかることはいくらでもある．そういう時は，「要約」という言葉にこだわりすぎずに，「要旨問題」だと見なして，筆者の主張と理由を書いて答案をつくればよい．実際に，要約と要旨の違いをあまり意識せずにつくられている設問もあるので，この違いにこだわりすぎないほうがよい場合がある．また，最初の1，2段落や最後の段落に全体のまとめ的な記述が入っていることもあるので，そういうところを利用してすばやく答案をつくれることもある．

解答

【解答例1】微生物は，人間や地球上の全生物にとって必要不可欠な役割を，複雑な微生

物群集の中ではたしている．しかし，顕微鏡の発明以来，微生物研究は，純粋培養された個々の微生物を実験室で研究するということに焦点を当ててきた．つまり，微生物に関する知識は，生態系という文脈を考慮せずに入手されたものだ．しかし，メタゲノム解析が誕生し，今後は微生物群集の中で生息している微生物を直接調べていけるので，顕微鏡の発明に端を発した変革と同じ程度の変革が起きるだろう．（219字）

【解説】
　第1段落は，最初に段落全体でいいたいことが提示されており，残りは具体例というシンプルな形になっている．具体的にいえば，第1段落は第4文まで読めば段落全体の内容がつかめる．よって第4文までを訳してまとめれば，第1段落の要約は終了である．残りの具体例は答案に入れる必要はない．要約問題では字数制限があるのが普通なので，具体例を答案に入れていると字数制限をオーバーしてしまう危険性が高い．よって具体例は，原則として答案に入れない方向で検討していくべきである．
　第2段落はどの文も重要である．全体を読んでまとめないといけない．注意点として，第1文と最終文はほぼ同じ内容と見てよい．よって，第1文と第2文をまとめればよい．まとめると，「微生物は，複雑な微生物群集の中で自分たちの役割をはたしているのに，微生物の研究は，純粋培養された単一の種だけに焦点を当ててきた」ということである．
　第3段落は，第3文以降が重要である．まず，第3文の文頭にある「thus」に注目したい．「thus」には，前言から導き出される結論を述べるという用法がある．訳としては，「したがって」「それゆえに」などでよい．結論を述べてくれているので，要約の際には注目したい単語である．第3文の内容を確認してみると，実は，第2段落の第2文とほぼ同じことを述べていることがわかる．これを受けて，第4文以降でまったく新しい内容が出てくるので注目してほしい．ようするに「これまでの微生物研究は，生態系を考慮せずに，実験室で純粋培養された単一の種に焦点を当ててきたが，メタゲノミクスの登場により，生態系を考慮に入れて，微生物を研究できるようになる」ということが述べられている．以上のことをふまえて要約を作成すればよいであろう．

【解答例2】　メタゲノミクスの登場で，生物学，医学，生態学，生物工学の世界では，顕微鏡の発明によって生じたのと同じくらい重大な変革が起こるであろう．なぜならば，メタゲノミクスにより，微生物を，それが普段くらしている生物群集の中にいる状態で調べることが可能になるからだ．微生物に関する従来の知識は，実験室で純粋培養された微生物を研究して得られた限定的なものであり，生態学的背景は全く無視されていたのだ．（193字）

【解説】
　これは【解答例1】と違って【3段落】だけに着眼した解答である．この英文は，ほとんど【3段落】に筆者のいいたいこととそれを述べるための道筋が出てきているので，結果的に【3段落】だけに着眼しても解答がほぼ書ける．ただし，ベストは【解答例1】である．

p.15【問題6】 鹿児島大学 平成20年

問題の特徴
　300字以内で遺伝子検査の問題点をまとめる問題である．問題点が書かれている箇所を見つけることは難しくない．見つけた後に，漏れなく問題点をまとめるという作業に時間をかけたい．

　なお，「○○字以内」と字数制限があるときには，「○○字」の少なくとも8割は超えていないといけないだろう．

本文のテーマ
　DTC型の遺伝子検査が問題となっている．遺伝医学に詳しい専門家・医療機関を通さず，直接消費者に遺伝学的検査サービスの提供を行う企業が現れた．このようなサービス提供は，様々な問題を引き起こす可能性が本文では指摘されている．

遺伝子検査とは
　遺伝性疾患などに関連した遺伝子型や遺伝子変異型を検出し，疾患の診断・治療または予防に役立てることである．なお，本文では，遺伝性疾患を対象にした遺伝子検査に焦点が当てられているが，感染症を診断するための遺伝子検査もとても重要である．

遺伝子検査に関連する事項
(1) 新生児スクリーニング

　出産後の新生児から血液を採取し，遺伝性疾患を早期に診断し，予防や治療につなげること．たとえば，新生児スクリーニングによりフェニルケトン尿症を発見できれば，食事療法により障害が生じるのを回避できる．しかし，出産後に異常がわかってもどうしようもないという疾患もある．そこで，もっと早い段階で胎児の異常を見つけたいという欲求が出てくる．こうして(2)の出生前診断に目が向けられるようになる．

(2) 出生前診断

　妊娠中に，子供の身体的・遺伝的状態を診断すること．染色体異常を調べるための羊水検査が典型例である．高齢出産の増加によって，近年は年間に約1万6000人が羊水検査を受けているといわれている．また最近では，妊婦の血液を調べるだけで胎児の染色体異常がわかるという検査が出てきている．羊水検査に比べ侵襲性が圧倒的に低いので注目されている．

(3) 着床前診断（または受精卵診断）

　体外受精によりつくられた受精卵の一部を採取し，遺伝子検査を行うもの．検査の結果，異常な遺伝子をもっていないことが判明した受精卵だけを，女性の子宮に戻すという目的

で行われる．倫理的な問題が大きい．日本産科婦人科学会は，重篤な遺伝性疾患に限り，学会で審議をし，承認された場合には，着床前診断を行ってよいという立場を取っている．

解答
【解答例】 ①新しい遺伝子検査により，遺伝的特徴が軽く扱われるようになる恐れがある．すべての遺伝子検査が認証を受けた研究施設で行われているわけではない．また，遺伝子検査の正確性や臨床的有効性に対する監視はほとんど，または，一切，行われていない．遺伝子検査の会社は，個人の生活習慣や家系のことを考慮していない．また，遺伝子検査で情報を得ても，行動に移せない場合がある．②疾患の決定的証拠となる遺伝子を特定することは難しいのに，企業が先走ってしまい，限られた情報によって，誤った安心感や恐怖感が生じるかもしれない．また，③医師は，遺伝子検査による遺伝情報の氾濫に対処するための準備ができていない．

【解説】
【4段落】から問題点の指摘がはじまっている点に注意．よって【4段落】以降から問題点を抜粋してまとめることになる．下線①が【4段落】で指摘されている問題点である．下線②は【5段落】をまとめたものである．下線③は【6段落】の最後から2つ目の文を参考にしている．これはぜひとも指摘しておきたい問題点であるが，見落としやすい．というのも【6段落】は前半で新しい遺伝子検査に対して肯定的な話が展開されており，一見すると，問題点が指摘されているような段落には見えないからである．

〔語句〕 oversight ＝監視　　　take O into account ＝ O を考慮に入れる
　　　　 odds ＝可能性　　　　translate … into action ＝…を実行に移す

【別解】 遺伝子検査は政府に認定された機関でのみ実施されている訳ではなく，検査の正確さや得られた情報の臨床医療での有効性に関する審査もない．また遺伝子情報を扱う企業の大部分が個人の将来の健康上のリスクを測る際，遺伝子の差異にのみ注目し，健康により強い関係性をもつ生活習慣上の要素を見落としている．さらに，医師の側ではこれらの遺伝子情報を医療に有効活用する準備がいまだ整っていない．したがって，人々は遺伝子情報ビジネスを行う企業から提供されるごく限られた遺伝子情報に基づいて，誤った健康管理に陥る危険性がある．また，実際の治療ではなく，単に情報を得ることに対し高額の医療費を払うことの是非も問われるべきである．

【解説】
　すべての問題点を指摘できているわけではないが，コンパクトにまとめている．接続詞等を使って，問題点を流れるように指摘している．

1.3　選択式問題

p.18【問題7】高知大学　平成17年

問題の特徴

　高知大学は本問のような選択式の問題を出題している．各選択肢の正誤判断を行う場合には，必ず根拠となる英文を1つ1つ本文から丁寧に見つけ出してほしい．いい加減な解き方をしていると実力はつかない．

　高知大学の問題は選択肢が多く，原則として消去法が使えない．全問正解を狙うよりも，解きやすい問題で確実に得点をすることがポイントになる．たとえば，問3のようにかなり迷ってしまうような問題もあるので，そういう問題はさっさと割り切って答えを出し，時間をロスしないようにしたい．

解答
問1　【解答例】3

【解説】
a　Semmelweisは医師の汚染された手指が患者に病気を広めている可能性にはじめて気づいた人物である．
　⇒×．【1段落】の第3文に反する．
b　医学生は助産師学生よりも手指の清潔を心がけていた．
　⇒×．【1段落】の第10文に反する．
c　たとえ手術用手袋を着用していても，外科手術を行っている医師の手指の常在菌が患部へ移行することが起こりうる．
　⇒○．【2段落】の第3文以降を読んでいけば正しいことがわかる．
d　21世紀になって，患者を診察する前に手洗いをしないような医師はいなくなった．
　⇒×．【3段落】の第4文に反する．

問2　【解答例】7

【解説】
a　病棟により死亡率に違いがあった．
　⇒関係が深い．【1段落】の第4文参照．
b　病棟により入院患者の社会的地位に違いがあった．
　⇒関係は深くない．【1段落】の第7文参照．
c　病棟により患者を担当する学生の専攻が異なった．

⇒関係は深い．【1段落】の第8文参照．
d 病棟によりベッドあたりの患者数に有意な差があった．
⇒関係は深くない．【1段落】の第8文参照．
e 病棟により患者担当学生の妊婦診察の頻度が違った．
⇒関係は深くない．【1段落】からは頻度が違ったかどうかははっきりわからない．

問3 【解答例】3

【解説】
　この問題は深く考えなければ，正解は3になる．しかし，細かい文法にこだわり出すと，正解にたどりつけなくなる．この問題は深く考えすぎて時間をロスしないことが大事である．興味のある人は以下の〔参考〕を読んでおいてほしい．
〔参考〕
　(②)には，意味だけを考えるなら undermines（～を損なわせる）が入ることは容易にわかる．しかし直前に，the surgeon was using mineral oil .... という過去形の文がきているので，それに合わせて undermined となるべきではないかという疑問が生じる．個人的には，そのように考えて正解を9にする人がいてもおかしくはないと思う．ただ，これだとあまりにもあっさりと答えが出てしまうので，出題者の立場に立つと，おそらくundermines が正解になるのであろう．「鉱油により外科手術用の手袋の完全性が損なわれる」というのは現在でも成り立つ普遍的事実なので，直前に過去形の文がきていようが，現在形を使って書いてもおかしくないと考えられる．
　(④)も少しまぎらわしいところがある．正解は is costing them（～に損害を与える）である．ただし，主語が2つある（the lack of hand washing と improper use of gloves）ので，is costing ではなく，are costing になるべきではないかという疑問が生じる．しかし，主語が2つあっても，それが一体化していると考えられる場合には，単数扱いをすることができる場合がある．たとえば，ham and eggs は，単数扱いできる場合がある．本問でも，筆者が the lack of hand washing と improper use of gloves を一体化して捉えていると考えれば，is costing になっていてもおかしくはない．ただ，筆者がこの2つを一体化して捉えていると見抜くことは難しいと思う．よって，ここも is costing ではおかしいと考えて，正解を9にする人がいてもおかしくないであろう．

問4 【解答例】1

【解説】
　aかeで少し迷うかもしれない．【3段落】は，1980年代だけでなく現在でも手術前の手洗いに対する認識が甘い医師がいるということを中心に述べている段落なので，選択肢eは，この段落の流れに合わないと考えるべきであろう．医師の手洗いに対する認識が甘

くても，病院の監視体制がよくなったので，手洗いを疎かにしている医師がいても，多くの感染者を出す前に発見されることになると考えたほうが，段落全体の趣旨に合致する．

問 5 【解答例】 4

【解説】
「Every cloud has a silver lining.（どんな雲も裏は銀色に輝いている）」という諺を知っているとわかりやすい．この諺は，「悪いことの反面には必ずよいことがある」という意味である．下線部（1）の「black cloud」は，この諺を元に考えると，悪いことを指している．そして this がついているので，その悪いことは直前に書かれているということになる．直前（【3段落】の最終文）を見ると，確かに悪いこと（手洗いを軽んずるような態度が病院の中でまだはびこっていた）が書かれている．

1.4 英作文

学士試験では，英作文が出題される大学は限られていると考えておいてよい．英作文が出題される有名な大学は，旭川医科，浜松医科，岡山，島根の4校であろう．この4校を受験する人は英作文の対策が特に必要となる．島根だけが和文英訳で，他の3校は，設問形式の違いはあるが，論述型の英作文である．

p.22【問題8】 旭川医科大学　平成17年

問題の特徴

旭川医科大学の英語は，長文読解と論述型英作文の2つから構成されている．本問もこの構成になっている．なお，最近では，長文読解の問題の中に内容一致問題が入るようになった．本文の内容に関する短文が8つほど書かれており，それぞれの内容が本文の内容と合致しているかどうかを判定する問題である．

旭川の読解問題は純粋な英語力が問われる．医学や生命科学の知識があれば，英語が苦手でも何とかできるという問題が学士試験ではけっこう出てくるが，旭川の英語はそうした感じではない．もっとも，旭川を受験する人の傾向を見ると，英語よりも生命科学の学力のほうが高いという人が多いので，英語が苦手な人でも敬遠する必要はない．

旭川の論述型英作文はしっかり対策しておく必要がある．英語で自分の意見を書くわけだが，シンプルな構成でわかりやすく書いておくことが重要．見たときに，どこに何が書いてあるかがすぐにわかるような答案がベストである．具体的には解答のところで説明する．

解答

問1 (1)【解答例】 合理的な患者であれば，明らかにこの情報が自分たちの意思決定に必要不可欠なものだとわかる．だから，真のインフォームドコンセントを得るには必ず，医学生を医者だとするのではなく，医学生という本当の身分を打ち明けなくてはいけない．

【解説】

下線部（A）：Since reasonable patients clearly ① find this information material to their decision, ② true informed consent cannot be obtained without disclosing the true status of medical students as students, not doctors.

下線部①は「find O C」という第5文型になっている．material が「重要である」という形容詞で使われている点に注意．下線部②は，文法的には二重否定構文といわれる形だが，そうしたことを知らなくても，普通に訳していけば何とかなるであろう．

(2) ①【解答例】 1つ目は，大学病院に入院することにしたということは，医学生による

治療を受けることに暗に同意していることになるということ．2つ目は，処置を行うのが医学生だということを知れば，患者に必要のないストレスや緊張感をもたらすということ．3つ目は，患者が学生による処置を拒否すれば，将来，他の患者が不十分な技術しか身につけていない医師の処置により苦しむことになるということ．

【解説】
【4段落】に (1) (2) (3) という番号がついている箇所がある．この部分を和訳すればよい．

(2) ②【解答例】 第1の正当化事由に対しては，大学病院への入院には，医学生が自分の治療に関与することへの同意は含まれていないと反論している．たいていの患者には選択の余地などなく，大学病院に入院せざるを得ないからだ．さらに，同意が前提であるならば，身分を偽ることなど必要ないはずだと指摘している．

また，第2の正当化事由に対しては次のように反論している．すなわち，医学生だと知らずに処置を受けて，後でそのことを知ったときに生じるストレスや不信感のほうが悪い影響をもたらすと指摘している．また，患者には，医学生の教育に関与するかどうかを決定する権利があり，それを適切に行使するには，医学生という身分をきちんと告げる必要があるともしている．

第3の正当化事由に対しては，これまでの研究から考えれば，医学生の身分を明かしても，研修に支障をきたさないほどの数の患者が，医学生の関与を進んで受け入れてくれるはずだと反論している．また，腰椎穿刺に関しては，正しい知識を普及させることで，医学生の関与に同意してくれる患者を増やせるとしている．

さらに，医学教育の負担は社会全体が負わなければならず，大学病院に入院した貧しい患者や無保険の患者だけが，その意に反して，医学生による初めての処置を受けなくてはいけないということではないとしている．

【解説】
字数制限がないので，どれくらい書けばよいのかがわかりづらい．ここでは，具体例などは極力削り，ポイントだけをまとめたつもりである．

【5段落】に【4段落】(1)への反論，【6段落】に【4段落】(2)への反論，【7段落】と【8段落】に【4段落】(3)への反論が書かれているということをきちんと確認してほしい．【7段落】は長いが，「Taking these studies into account, approximately one-third or more of patients may be willing to allow students to perform spinal taps in non-emergency settings.」というまとめ的な文や，「Moreover, some of the patients' apprehension regarding spinal taps, may be due to a commonly held, but false, belief that spinal taps carry a high risk of paralysis.」という追加情報をつけ足す文に着眼して読めばまとめやすい．

(3)【解答例】 医学生は，指導教官との関係と，患者との関係の中で自分の役割や義務を

吟味しなくてはいけないとしている．そしてこれらの関係においては信頼が最も大切な要素であり，医学生は信頼を維持し，最大化するような行動をとるべきであるとしている．具体的には，医師として紹介された場合には，いったん指導医とともに部屋から出て，指導医に医療を学ぶ機会を作ってもらったことへの感謝と自分の新しい医療措置への学習意欲を述べた上で，患者が，自分が学生であることに後で気づいたら，自分のみならず指導医も信頼を失うかもしれないという不安を述べるべきだとしている．こうすることで指導教官から肯定的な反応が得られ，学生はリスクを最小化できると筆者は指摘している．

【解説】
　まずは下線部 (C) の直後の文をふまえることが大切である．この文では，指導教官 (mentor) との関係と患者との関係の両方に配慮する必要性が述べられている．そして，それらの関係において重要な要素となるのは信頼であるとの記述が，最後から3つ目の段落の冒頭で述べられている．そして，この信頼を維持するために具体的にどうすればよいかが，最後から2つ目の段落で述べられている．こうした流れをふまえればよい．

問2
論述型英作文の注意点

1. まずは，設問を丁寧に読み，何を論述する必要があるのかをしっかり確認する．これをうっかりして，設問で問われていないことを論述してしまうと高得点は望めない．
2. 全体の流れがわかりやすい答案を目指す．英語を日本語と同じくらい自由に使える人以外は，趣向を凝らした構成にする必要はない．採点官が答案を見たらどこに何が書いてあるかがすぐにわかることが望ましい．【解答例1】【解答例2】のように，【1段落】を見れば，その後の展開が予測できる答案がよい．【1段落】がわかりにくい答案は，採点官の印象が悪くなり，高得点は望めない．流れがわかりやすい答案だと印象がよくなり，多少文法的なミスがあっても多めに見てもらえる可能性も出てくる．
3. 論述型の問題では，自分の意見を求められることが圧倒的に多いが，その際には，その理由を必ず示すこと．理由を示すとは，自分の意見の根拠となる事実や具体例を示すことだと考えてほしい．自分の主観や感情を理由付けに使ってはいけない．理由の個数は3つが望ましいが，あまりこだわる必要はない．状況に応じて調節してほしい．時間がない，いい理由が浮かばないなどの事情があれば，1つか2つにとどめてもよい．
4. 自分の知っている構文を駆使して，または，できるだけ簡単な単語を使って誤りがない文を書くこと．たとえば，「学校の衛生状態を維持することが大切である」という日本語が答案作成の際に頭に浮かんだとしよう．露骨に英訳すると，「It is important to maintain the sanitary conditions of schools.」となる．しかし，よく考えてみると，「It is important to keep schools clean.」と簡単に書いてもよいのである．前者のような英訳しかできないと，単語のスペルミスなどが生じてくる恐れがある．後者のように簡単な単語を使うことができれば，間違いを減らせるであろう．もう少し別の言い方

をすれば，前者のように自分の頭に浮かんだ日本語をストレートに英語に直そうとすると，危険な場合があるということである．

【解答例 1】肯定の立場（番号は解説のために付した）

【1段落】 ① I think that doctors can practice medicine and carry out research without violating the 'do no harm' rule. ② Genetic testing and euthanasia are good examples to support this opinion.

【2段落】 ③ Genetic testing means checking whether a person has defective genes related to diseases.　④ If genetic testing tells you that you have genetic defects that cause Alzheimer's disease, you are very shocked and may get into depression because there is no cure for the disease. In this case, genetic testing does harm to you.　⑤ But, it is possible to perform genetic testing without doing any harm. You can or must usually consult a genetic counselor or a doctor before you take genetic testing. The counselor or the doctor informs you of all important information such as the benefits or risks of genetic testing. The information will make it possible for you to avoid genetic test(ing)s that are harmful for you. When genetic testing is combined with genetic counseling, this testing is compatible with the 'do no harm' rule.

【3段落】 ⑥ Euthanasia means killing without pain a terminal patient with an incurable disease who suffers from unbearable pain. ⑦ Judging from this definition, it seems clear that euthanasia violates the 'do no harm' rule. ⑧ But, there are some cases when euthanasia is not against this rule. For example, it is wrong to keep on performing futile medical treatments on terminal patients with no hope of recovery against their wishes. In this case, the futile medical treatments do harm to them, because the treatments invade their dignity and their autonomy. So, performing euthanasia is not always against the 'do no harm' rule.

【4段落】 ⑨ The above examples show that doctors can practice medicine and carry out research without violating the 'do no harm' rule. Doctors must continue to provide patients with proper medical treatments based on this rule.

【解説】

①まず自分の意見を表明している．なお，自分の意見を書く時は原則として「I think that …」という表現は使わないほうがよい．「…」の部分だけを書けばよい．ここでは，設問が「Do you think doctors can practice medicine and carry out research … ?」となっているので，それに合わせているだけである．

②自分の意見を補強する例を2つ（【2段落】で genetic testing,【3段落】で euthanasia）提示している．このようなシンプルな構成をとるのがよい．ようするに，【1段落】を

読めば文全体の構造が予測できるようになっている．
③定義を述べている．このように定義を入れておくと読みやすい．
④⑤いったん反対の立場に言及する．その後，butという接続詞を使って自分の立場を表明する．この流れはよく出てくるので参考にしてほしい．
⑥定義を述べている．
⑦⑧反対の立場から自分の立場へという流れ．【2段落】と同じパターンで書いている．
⑨まとめの段落である．

【解答例2】否定の立場

【1段落】　① I think that it is very difficult for doctors to practice medicine and carry out research without violating this part of the Hippocratic Oath. ② There are two examples to support this opinion.

【2段落】　③ First, I want to take genetic testing for example. ④ Genetic testing means examining whether you have defective genes related to diseases. ⑤ In some cases, genetic testing can benefit you. ⑥ However, genetic testing does great harm to you if genetic testing shows you that you have a gene for Alzheimer's disease. This is because there is no cure for the disease. In addition, I am concerned that the number of companies selling genetic testing kits is increasing. You can easily buy these kits off the Internet, examine your genes, and know your own genetic information related to diseases. But, the information can cause much fear unless you know how to use it properly. What is worse, there are some genetic testing kits whose accuracy is very low. This is why some people may obtain from the kits inaccurate genetic information that can do harm.

【3段落】　⑦ Second, I want to take gene therapy for example. ⑧ Gene therapy means inserting normal genes into a patient's cell to replace defective genes or absent genes. ⑨ In inserting normal genes, scientists use altered viruses, because viruses have an ability to insert their genes into a host's genome. But, altered viruses can stimulate a patient's immune system excessively and cause inflammation and, in some cases, organ failure. In addition, genes inserted by altered viruses may disturb a patient's genome and cause cancer. In addition, I have heard the news that a volunteer who participated in a clinical trial of gene therapy died suddenly during the trial. Gene therapy has a lot of potential harm that patients cannot avoid.

【4段落】　Two examples show that it is hard for doctors to practice medicine and carry out research without violating this part of the Hippocratic Oath.

【解説】
①自分の意見を表明している．
②ここでは，例が2つあることだけを示しており，例の中身までは述べていない．

③ 1つ目の例を First という言葉を使ってあげている．
④ 遺伝子診断の定義を述べている．
⑤⑥「反対の立場 → 逆接の接続詞 → 自分の立場」という流れをつくっている．
⑦ 2つ目の例を Second という言葉を使ってあげている．
⑧ 遺伝子治療の定義を述べている．
⑨ 定義を使って遺伝子治療の問題点を述べている．

〔補足〕
　設問では「abortion」「cloning」「organ transplants」「physician-assisted suicide」といった項目もリストアップされていたので，少しコメントしておく．

1　abortion を答案に使う場合に参考になる表現
・Abortion means preventing a fetus from being born alive.
・Abortion means ending a pregnancy by artificial means.
・Doctors cannot carry out an abortion without violating the "do no harm" rule, because this practice involves the act of killing a fetus.（involve は「伴う」という意味）

2　cloning を答案に使う場合に参考になる表現
・Cloning means making an organism that is genetically identical to another.
・Cloning means making a genetically identical copy of an individual.（individual ＝ 個体）
・It is said that some scientists carry out research on cloning a human by nuclear transfer, which means putting the nucleus of a person's body cell into a human egg cell whose nucleus has been removed.
・Animals cloned by nuclear transfer show a variety of health problems. For example, Dolly the sheep, the first cloned mammal, suffered from arthritis at a relatively young age.
・Cloned humans are likely to suffer from the health problems that humans born through normal processes do not have.

3　organ transplants を答案に使う場合に参考になる表現
・Organ transplants mean putting a person's organ into another. Organ transplant is divided into two types: transplants from the deceased and ones from living donors. Taking organs from a dead person does no harm, as long as the practice is performed according to right laws or rules. It is true that living donor transplants may expose living donors to risk. But, doctors have a lot of precise knowledge about living donor transplants and can avoid transplants that may do great harm to living donors. In addition, remarkable progress in medical skills related to transplants has enabled doctors to perform safer living donor transplants. This is why organ transplants don't violate the 'do no harm' rule.

- Before the 1980s, organ transplants were very dangerous. Recipients suffered from organ rejections and some of them died. In the 1980s, the drug that makes organ rejections less severe was developed. This drug has made organ transplants less dangerous to organ recipients.

4　physician-assisted suicide を答案に使う場合に参考になる表現
- Physician-assisted suicide means that a physician helps a patient commit suicide. Judging from this definition, this act seems to violate the 'do no harm' rule. But, physician-assisted suicide may not be against this rule, if a doctor performs it according to a request from a patient who has an incurable disease, suffers from unbearable pain, and have little time to live.

【参考】次のようなシンプルな答案の書き方も参考にしてほしい．
Read the following, and write your opinion in English.

　　Currently patients pay user fees of 30% when using healthcare services in Japan. It has been suggested that these fees need to be raised to pay for the increasing costs of healthcare. Argue for or against this proposal. Support your argument with reasons and examples.（旭川医科大学　平成21年）

【解答例】

① For two reasons, the user fees of 30% that patients pay don't need to be raised.

② The first reason is that raising the user fees increases medical costs more. Some people say that raising the user fees leads to curbing medical costs, but this is wrong. If user fees are raised, more and more people of low income will refrain from going to see a doctor, unless they become very ill. As a result, doctors will have to treat a lot of very ill people. This will increase medical costs.

③ The second reason is that there are some other ways to reduce the increasing costs of healthcare. For example, the government and doctors can advise people to change unhealthy lifestyles. Now, the number of people who get lifestyle-related diseases is increasing and this is increasing medical costs. If people change their bad lifestyles, medical costs will gradually begin to decrease. Therefore, there will be no need to raise user fees.

　For the above reasons, it is wrong to raise the user fees of 30%. That produces the opposite effect. We have some ways to reduce the increasing costs of healthcare.

【解説】
①2つ理由があることを示す．とても簡単な書き方になっている．
②③1つ目と2つ目の理由を，わかりやすいように段落を分けて順番に示している．

p.28【問題9】 浜松医科大学　平成15年

問題の特徴

　典型的な和文英訳の問題である．英作文でよく使われる基本例文を暗記していることが，こうした問題を解くための前提となる．また，与えられた和文を直訳しようとせずに，英語に直しやすいように多少加工することも必要である．与えられた和文を，一度，別の和文に直してから，それを英語に直すという感じである．また，今述べたこととほぼ同じことだが，和文を100%忠実に英訳しようとしないほうがよい場合が多い．肩の力を抜いて，和文の内容の70〜80%くらいを英訳するつもりで取り組むとよい．もっといえば，自分が正確に使える英語表現で書けるところだけを確実に解答しておくという発想でもいいくらいである．

　なお，近年の浜松医科大学では，このような和文英訳型の問題が消えつつある．最近は読解型の英作問題に変わってきている．英語の長文を読み，本文の核心的な内容に関する問いに，英語で答えるという問題になってきている．問いは1問だけであり，語数は150語ほど要求される．まずは，普通の内容説明問題と同じように，解答に必要な箇所を探すことが大事である．その後，その箇所に出てきている英文を丸写しして解答を作成できれば一番楽であるが，「本文の丸写しはいけない」という指示がなされていることが多い．よって，自分で少し英文を書き換えて答案化しないといけない．本文に出ている表現をすべて書き換えると時間がかかるので，小規模な書き換えでよいであろう．たとえば，「He worked hard to support his family.」を「He worked hard so that he could support his family.」というふうに書き換えるくらいでもよいだろう．参考にしてほしい．

解答

【解答例1】 ① From such a viewpoint, science has to be understood by everyone and a scientific experiment has to produce the same result, no matter who performs it. ② In short, science has to be objective. ③ In order to achieve this, a scientific thesis has to include arguments and reasoning that are based on precise theories. ④ In addition, the results have to be confirmed by observations and experiments.

【解説】

① 「…再現できることが必須の条件である」は，「…再現できなければならない」と考える．「誰がおこなっても」は，「no matter who S V」の構文を使いたい．知らなければ，「even if anyone performs it」という形を使うことになる．

② 「客観性が保証されねばならない」は，「客観的でなければいけない」と考えて英訳する．

③ 「科学の論文はまちがいのない理論にしたがって議論と推論をおこない…」を，「a scientific thesis must argue and reason according to precise theories」と直訳するのは不自然な感じがする．直訳せずに，「科学の論文は，まちがいのない理論に基づい

た議論と推論を含む」と言い換えて英訳するとよい．または，「科学論文においては，著者は，まちがいのない理論にしたがって議論と推論をおこない…」と言い換えて英訳することも考えられる．この場合には，「In a scientific thesis, the author has to argue and reason based on precise theories.」という英訳になるであろう．

④ In addition という言葉を使って，2文(③と④)に分けている．和文では1文であっても，英語に直すときは2文に分けてよい．このように分けたほうが楽に書ける場合がよく出てくる．

【解答例2】（できるだけ和文に忠実に解答した場合）
From such a viewpoint, ① it is an essential condition that science is understood by everyone and that a scientific experiment produces the same result, no matter who performs it. In short, ② objectiveness has to be guaranteed in science. ③ To that end, a scientific thesis has to include arguments and reasoning that are based on precise theories. In addition, the results have to be ④ verified by observations and experiments.

【解説】
① it が形式主語で，真主語が that 節以下である．和文に忠実だが，くどい書き方である．条件という単語を忘れた人は，「It is essential that S V…」という書き方にしておけばよい．いずれにせよ，【解答例1】のように書いた方が明らかに簡潔である．
② 「guarantee（保証する）」を使っている．しかし，この単語は英作文の際に頻繁に使用する基本単語とまではいえないであろう．無理をしてスペルミスをするくらいなら，【解答例1】のような発想で書いた方がよい．
③ 「to that end（そのために）」という熟語を知っていて，なおかつ，英作文でも自由に使えるレベルになっている人はそうはいないであろう．
④ 「verify（立証する，実証する）」という単語を知っていれば楽である．しかし，できればこのような難しめの単語は使いたくないところである．

p.29【問題 10】 島根大学 平成 22 年

問題の特徴

　島根大学は，毎年必ず本問のような和文英訳型の問題を出す．語注がほとんどないのでかなり苦しそうに見える．たとえば本問の 3) では「敗血症」という単語が出てくるが，ほとんどの人が書けないであろう．ほとんどの人ができないということは，あまり気にしなくてよいということである．ようするに 100% 英訳できる必要はない．自分の知っている表現で書ける部分だけを確実に書いて，部分点を狙うことが大切である．英作文の他に読解問題が 3 題出るが，まず英作文の問題を見て，書けるところをさっと書いてしまい，その後，読解問題に取り組むというやり方が定番になっている．

　島根大学のような和文英訳の問題では，減点法で採点がなされるのが普通なので，明らかなミスをしないように注意してほしい．特に大きな減点対象となるものをいくつか挙げておく．

(1) 動詞の使い方にミスがあり，文が成立していない．

例：An earthquake arises much damage.

→×：arise は「生じる」という意味の自動詞であり，目的語をとらない動詞である．arise の代わりに cause を使えば正しい文がつくれる．cause は「引き起こす」という意味の他動詞である．

(2) 受動態の誤用

例：He was stolen his car.

→×：日本人の感覚からすれば，この文は「彼は，彼の車を盗まれた」という意味の正しい文のように見える．しかし，steal には，4 文型の用法がないので，「be + done + 名詞」という形の受動態はつくれない．4 文型を作れる give の場合と比較してほしい．「He was given a new drug.」は，「彼は新薬を投与された」という意味の正しい文となる．

(3) 品詞を無視した書き方

例：Cats are differ from dogs.

→×：differ は動詞なので，正しくは different という形容詞を使うべきである．

例：He knows a lot about the world despite he is young.

→×：despite は前置詞なので，直後に文は置けない．接続詞である though を使って「though he is young.」とすべきである．前置詞と接続詞を混同してはいけない．

(4) 文と文をコンマだけでつないではいけない．

例：The doctor gave me some medicines, they had no effect on me.

→×：文と文をコンマだけでつないでいる．これは英作文の答案では絶対に避けたい間違いである．they の前に but という接続詞を入れてほしい．文と文をつなぐときは接続詞を使う．

(5) because の誤用

例：We are concerned about obesity. Because the number of obese people is increasing now.

→×:「because SV〜」だけを単独で使うことは避けること．このミスをする人は非常に多い．これはくだけた表現であり，英作文では減点される．正しくは，「We are concerned about obesity, because the number of obese people is increasing now.」となる．または「We are concerned about obesity. This is because the number of obese people is increasing now.」でもよい.

解答

1)【解答例1】 Since electronic microscopes were developed, scientists have become able to observe deeper parts of the natural world through them than they did through normal light microscopes.

【解答例2】 The development of electronic microscopes has allowed scientists to observe deeper parts of the natural world than they did through normal light microscopes.

【解説】
　解答例1は，できるだけ和文に忠実に英訳したものである．解答例2は，和文を加工して，無生物主語を使って書いている．無生物主語を使うとすっきりとしたよい答案が書ける場合がしばしばある．「allow O to do … ＝ O が…するのを可能にする」という形は，必ず使えるようにしてほしい．

2)【解答例】Influenza is an infectious respiratory disease caused by influenza viruses. Influenza causes mild to severe diseases. It sometimes kills people.

【解説】
　この問題は和文を加工する必要はほとんどない．あとは単語をどれだけ知っているかということになる．

3)【解答例1】 According to a study, infectious diseases such as pneumonia, diarrhea, malaria, and sepsis cause more than two thirds of the 8,800,000 annual deaths of children under five years old in the world.

【解答例2】 In the world, 8,800,000 children die under five years old every year. A study shows that more than two thirds of the deaths are caused by infectious diseases such as pneumonia, diarrhea, malaria, and sepsis.

【解説】
【解答例1】は和文にできるだけ忠実に書いたものである．しかし，下線部が少し窮屈な

書き方になっている．これを嫌うなら【解答例2】のようにしてもよい．【解答例2】は「世界では，毎年，5歳未満の子供が8,800,000人死んでいる．ある研究によれば，このうち3分の2以上は，肺炎，下痢，マラリア，敗血症といった感染症によって引き起こされている」という和文に加工してから英訳したものである．

敗血症という難しい単語が出てきているが，知らなければ無視して，「肺炎，下痢，マラリア」だけを英訳しておけばよい．「知らなければ無視」という発想が大切である．敗血症のことをよく知っている人なら，「a diseased condition caused by microbes or their toxins in the blood」というふうに説明的に書くこともできるであろう．しかし，本問ではこの説明的な書き方を使うと，すなわち【解答例1】と【解答例2】のsepsisのところにこの説明的な書き方を代入すると，やや読みづらい英文になると思われる．

なお，「肺炎」「下痢」「マラリア」という単語は書ける人がいても全然おかしくない．ここは差が出るであろう．

〔語句〕肺炎＝ pneumonia　　　下痢＝ diarrhea　　　敗血症＝ sepsis, blood poisoning
〔参考〕ユニセフ（国連児童基金）によると，2006年における世界の5歳未満児の死亡は年間970万人にのぼる．

4)【解答例1】 Ten percent of the body fluid filtered by capillary vessels when blood moves from arteries to veins accumulates in body tissues with proteins essential for life. This body fluid loss will promptly expose life to risk if the lymphatic system does not work properly.

【解答例2】 Ten percent of the body fluid filtered by capillary vessels <u>during the passage of the blood from arteries to veins</u> remains in body tissues with proteins needed to sustain life. This body fluid loss can be promptly life-threatening if the lymphatic system does not function correctly.

【解説】

単語力があれば，ほぼ直訳でいける．percentは複数形にしない．「数字 percent of 名詞 」が主語の場合，動詞は 名詞 の数に呼応する．【解答例1】では，the body fluidが単数なので，動詞もそれに合わることになる（【解答例2】も同様）．【解答例2】の下線の書き方は，なかなか浮かばないであろう．無理せずに，【解答例1】のように書けばよい．

〔語句〕毛細血管＝ capillary vessel　　　リンパ系＝ lymphatic system

★英作文用に覚えてほしい例文集 1

1	ゴミを燃やすとダイオキシンが発生するということはよく知られている．	It is well known that burning garbage produces dioxin.
2	この研究は，絶滅危惧種が絶滅するのを防ぐうえで重要な役割をはたしている．	This study plays an important role in preventing endangered species from becoming extinct.
3	脳死と植物状態を区別することは重要である．	It is important to distinguish brain death from vegetative state.
4	人体がどのように機能するのかを理解するためには，化学に関する基礎的な知識が必要である．	In order to understand how the human body works, you need to have a basic knowledge of chemistry.
5	これにより，酵素が，何度も同じことをくり返し行うことが可能になる．	This allows the enzyme to do the same thing over and over again.
6	私たちは，人間が想像以上に他の哺乳類と似ているということを認識するようになった．	We have come to realize that humans are more similar to other mammals than we imagined.
7	この情報を基にしてこの計画を拒否するかどうかを決めなければいけない．	We have to decide whether to reject the plan based on this information.
8	動物に抗生物質を使っていると，耐性菌が生まれるかもしれないという懸念がある．	There is concern that using antibiotics on animals may create resistant bacteria.
9	実験動物の福祉は，尊重されなければならない．	The welfare of animals used for research must be respected.
10	理由はどうあれ，医師による自殺幇助は違法である．	No matter what the reason is, it is illegal for doctors to help their patients kill themselves.
11	働きすぎで，私は頭痛になった．	Too much work gave me a headache.
12	クローン技術は二つに分類される．生殖型クローンと治療型クローンである．	Cloning technology can be divided into two types: reproductive and therapeutic cloning.
13	あなたの体細胞の一つ一つには，23組の染色体が含まれている．組になっている染色体のうちの1本は，父親から，残りのもう1本は，母親から受けついだものだ．	You have 23 pairs of chromosomes in each one of your body cells. One of each pair came from your father and the other one from your mother.

14	ある国の紙の消費量と，その国の文化水準との間には密接な関係がある．	The amount of paper consumed by a country is closely related to the cultural standard of it. 【別解】 There is a close relationship between the amount of paper consumed by a country and the cultural standard of it.
15	結婚しても名字を変えたくないという女性が増えている．	The number of women who say that they don't want to change their family names after marriage is increasing. 【別解1】 More and more women say that they don't want to change their surnames after marriage. 【別解2】 There is an increase in the number of women who say that they don't want to change their family names after marriage.
16	メディケイドの適用を受けている子供が精神病治療薬を処方される可能性は，民間の保険の適用を受けている子供たちの4倍である．＊精神病治療薬＝antipsychotic drugs	Children covered by Medicaid are four times more likely to get antipsychotic drugs than those covered by private insurers.
17	この本は，思っていたよりも面白い．	This book is more interesting than I expected.
18	日本ほど地震の多い国はない．	No other country in the world has more earthquakes than Japan. 【別解1】 Japan has more earthquakes than any other country in the world. 【別解2】 Japan has the most earthquakes in the world.
19	年を取ればとるほど，記憶力は悪くなる．	The older you get, the weaker your memory becomes.
20	若者の活字離れが進んでいる．	Young people don't read as (so) many books as they did before.

【例文集1の解説】

1　① It is well known that ② burning garbage produces dioxin.
【解説】
①形式主語の it.
②動名詞で主語をつくるパターン．

2　This study ① plays an important role in ② preventing endangered species from becoming extinct.
【解説】
①「重要な役割をはたす」という意味でとても重要．
② prevent O from doing … ＝ O が…するのを妨げる

3　It is important to distinguish brain death from vegetative state.
【解説】形式主語 it の構文．「distinguish A from B ＝ A と B を区別する」も重要．

4　In order to understand how the human body works, you need to have a basic knowledge of chemistry.
【解説】下線部は目的を表わす不定詞．in order はなくてもよい．

5　This allows the enzyme to do the same thing over and over again.
〔語句〕allow O to do … ＝ O が…するのを許す，O が…することを可能にする

6　We have come to realize that humans are more similar to other mammals than we imagined.
【解説】「come to do … ＝ …するようになる」が重要．「be similar to … ＝ …に似ている」もしっかり覚えてほしい．「be different from … ＝ …と異なっている」も覚えること．
〔参考〕Cats are different from dogs in the way they behave. 犬と猫は，行動の仕方が違う．
　⇒この例文も覚えること．

7　We have to decide whether to reject the plan based on this information.
〔語句〕based on … ＝ …に基づいて

8　There is concern that using antibiotics on animals may create resistant bacteria.
【解説】「There is concern that S V … ＝ …という懸念がある」が重要．下線部は動名詞が主語をつくっている部分．

9   The welfare of animals underlined{used for research} must be respected.
【解説】下線部は過去分詞の形容詞用法できわめて重要．確実に使えるようにすること．

その他の参考例文
① We can avoid the problems related to the derivation of stem cells from human embryos.
私たちは，幹細胞をヒトの胚から取り出すことに関連する諸問題を回避できる．
② E-mail is a system designed to send messages and pictures by using personal computers linked to the Internet.
電子メールは，インターネットに接続されているパソコンを使ってメッセージや写真を送るために設計されたシステムです．

10   No matter what the reason is, it is illegal for doctors to help their patients kill themselves.
【解説】下線部の形が重要．

〔参考〕no matter 疑問詞節

(1) No matter what other people say, I will support organ transplants from brain-dead people.
(2) No matter who performs a surgery, aseptic techniques must be observed.
(3) No matter where you live, you are likely to be contaminated by trace amounts of POPs.   *POPs = persistent organic pollutants（残留性有機汚染物質）
(4) No matter what surgery you have there will always be an element of risk.
(5) I am a microbiologist working in a large hospital. No matter how careful I am, there is always the danger of infection in this work.
(6) However hard you study English, you cannot master it in a day.
(7) In this case, surgery is the better option, no matter how long it takes to get back to your regular life.
(8) No matter what the pathogen of the disease is, it comes out of hiding every few centuries.   *come out of hiding ＝現れる
(9) A scientific experiment, no matter how spectacular the results, is not completed until the results are published.

(1) たとえ他人が何といっても，私は脳死者からの臓器移植を支持するつもりである．
(2) たとえ誰が手術を行うにせよ，無菌法を遵守しなくてはいけない．
(3) あなたがどこに住んでいようが，微量のPOPsによる害を受ける可能性がある．
(4) どんな手術を受けるにせよ，いつも危険という要素がつきまとうかもしれない．

(5) 私は大病院で働いている微生物学者である．この仕事では，私がどんなに注意深くてもいつも感染という危険がつきまとう．
(6) どんなに一生懸命英語を勉強しても，1日でマスターすることはできない．
(7) この場合には，いつもの生活に戻るまでにどれだけ時間がかかろうが，手術を選択したほうがよい．
(8) その病気の病原体が何であろうとも，（とにかく）その病気は数世紀ごとに現れるのだ．
(9) 科学実験は，その結果がどんなに素晴らしいものであろうとも，その結果が（論文として）発表されるまでは，完了したとはいえないのだ．

⇒「no matter 疑問詞節」の「matter」には，「重要」という意味がある．そうすると，「no matter＝重要度ゼロ」ということ．つまり，この構文は，「疑問詞節の内容の重要度がゼロ」だといっていることになる．これをもう少しくだけた形でいうと，「疑問詞節の内容なんてどうでもいいよ」という感じになる．この感覚をもとに，手持ちの文法書を参考にしながら，上記の例文の意味をしっかり確認しておいてほしい．

11　Too much work gave me a headache.
【解説】無生物主語の構文．
〔参考〕「働きすぎて頭痛になった」は「I had a headache because I worked too much.」とも書ける．しかし無生物を主語にして「Too much work gave me a headache.」と書いたほうが文が引き締まるし，動詞の使用回数が減らせるので間違える確率が減る．

12　Cloning technology can be divided into two types : reproductive and therapeutic cloning.
【解説】分類する時の表現．

13　You have 23 pairs of chromosomes in each one of your body cells. One of each pair came from your father and the other one from your mother.
【解説】one と the other の関係を文法書でしっかり確認しておくこと．頻出する形である．

14　The amount of paper consumed by a country is closely realted to the cultural standard of it.
【別解】There is a close relationship between the amount of paper consumed by a country and the cultural standard of it.
【解説】関係性を語るための有名な表現．
〔語句〕have a connection with … ＝…と関連がある
have nothing to do with … ＝…と何の関係もない
There is no direct relationship between A and B ＝ A と B の間には直接の関係はない

15　The number of women who say that they don't want to change their family names after marriage is increasing.
【別解1】More and more women say that they don't want to change their surnames after marriage.
【別解2】There is an increase in the number of women who say that they don't want to change their family names after marriage.
【解説】増減表現が重要である．英作文の問題でよく出てくる．この3つの言い方をしっかり覚えること．

16　Children covered by Medicaid are four times more likely to get antipsychotic drugs than those covered by private insurers.
【解説】倍数表現．「倍数　比較級　than」という形になる．「倍数 as ～ as」という形でもよい．2倍は twice，3倍からは「three times」などのように time を使う．ただし twice は「倍数 as ～ as」の時にしか使わない．

17　This book are more interesting than I expected.
【解説】「思ったよりも」という表現が大切．「than I thought」でもよい．

18　No other country in the world has more earthquakes than Japan.
【別解1】Japan has more earthquakes than any other country in the world.
【別解2】Japan has the most earthquakes in the world.
【解説】最上級を，比較級を使って述べるための表現．

19　The older you get, the weaker your memory becomes.
【解説】ザヒザヒ構文「The 比較級 SV ～ , the 比較級 SV … ＝ ～すればするほどそれだけ…」
例文 19 は，「As you grow older, your memory becomes weaker.」とほぼ同じ意味になる．しかし，ザヒザヒ構文のほうが，比較級が文頭に出て目立つので，「～すればするほどもっと…」という関係性がより強調されることにはなる．しかし，比較級が本来の位置から離れて文頭に出るので，文構造は複雑になる．よって，自信がなければ，ザヒザヒ構文を回避し，こちらの as を使った形で書いておくのが無難である．

参考例文
① The longer you stay in America, the more difficult you find it to get along with American people.
　　アメリカに長くいればいるほど，アメリカ人とうまくやっていくことが難しいということがわかる．
② The harder you study medical science, the greater contribution you can make to

the society you live in.
医学を一生懸命勉強すればするほど，それだけ社会に大きな貢献ができる．

③ The more similar the cultural backgrounds of two people, the better able they will be to understand each other.
2人の人の文化的な背景が似ていれば似ているほど，それだけお互いをよりよく理解できる．
⇒ people の後に are が省略されている．

20　Young people don't read as（so）many books as they did before.
〔語句〕not as 原級 as … ＝…ほど～でない

★英作文用に覚えてほしい例文集 2

1	晩婚化のために，夫婦が育てる子供の数が減っている．	Because people tend to get married later in life, the number of children that couples raise is becoming smaller than before. 【別解】Because there is a tendency to get married later in life, the number of children that couples raise is becoming smaller than before.
2	新たな治療方法（therapies）が確立されるまでには，多くの基礎研究がなされる．	We have to perform a lot of basic studies before we establish a new therapy. 【別解】It takes a lot of basic studies to establish a new treatment.
3	多くの神経変性疾患が，特定のタンパク質の処理がうまくいかないことで引き起こされているということが明らかになってきている．	It is becoming clear that many neurodegenerative diseases are caused by improper protein processing.
4	日本の人口は 2006 年には減少しはじめると予想されている．そしてこの減少が続けば，2100 年には日本の人口は今の半分になるとされている． 　＊半減する＝decrease by half	It is estimated that Japan's population will start decreasing in 2006. If this decrease continues, Japan's population will get half as large in 2100 as it is now.
5	私があなたを捨てて別の男に走った理由は，あなたが優柔不断だということだ．	The reason why I left you for another man is that you are indecisive.

6	ある研究により，この物質が血圧を下げるのに役立つことがわかっている．	A study shows that this substance helps make blood pressure low.
7	2003年になってようやくヒトゲノムの全塩基配列が突き止められた．	It was only in 2003 that we finished sequencing the human genome.
8	前に得られているデータと比べると，今回の結果は理論計算の値とよく一致している．	Compared with the previous data, this result is compatible / consistent with theoretical values.
9	多くの病気の診断は，胸部X線検査に基づいて下されるかもしれない．	Many diseases may be diagnosed based on a chest X-ray test.
10	彼は，障害者に対して，彼らが生計を立てるために使える技術を教えている．	He teaches people with disabilities skills they can use to earn a living.
11	抜き打ちテストとは，学生が勉強しているかどうかを確かめるために，先生が何の予告もなしに実施する短いテストのことである．	A pop quiz means a short test that a teacher gives without any warning, in order to check whether students have been studying.
12	英語を習得できるかどうかは3つの要素にかかってくる．	Whether we can master English depends on three factors.
13	女性に中絶が必要なのかどうかが議論の的となっている．	Whether women need an abortion is a controversial topic.
14	貧血とは，通常よりも赤血球の数が少ないときに生じる，一般的な血液疾患である．	Anemia is a common blood disorder that occurs when there are fewer red blood cells than normal.
15	もし脳が我々に理解できるほど単純なものであれば，我々はそれを理解できないほど単純なものになるだろう．	If the brain were so simple we could understand it, we would be so simple we couldn't.
16	君が電話してくれなかったら，私は寝すごしていただろう．	If you had not called me, I would have overslept.
17	血液中の栄養分の量を十分な状態に維持するということだけでなく，血液中の老廃物や毒素を除去することも重要である．	It is important not only to maintain adequate nutrient levels in the blood, but also to eliminate wastes and toxins.

18 スマートフォンは私たちの日々の生活に必要不可欠である．	Smartphones are essential to our daily life.
19 猫と犬では行動の仕方が違う．	Cats are different from dogs in the way they behave.
20 これからの医療専門家は生活習慣病に焦点を当てていかねばならない．	Medical professionals in the future will have to focus on lifestyle-related diseases.
21 原子核は，たいてい1個かそれ以上の陽子といくつかの中性子とからできている．	The atomic nucleus is usually composed of one or more protons and some neutrons.
22 日本は石油を外国に依存している	Japan depends on foreign countries for oil.
23 最近ではワクチンを投与された人が増えているので，麻疹（ウイルス）にさらされることはめったにありません．	These days, people are rarely exposed to measles due to the high number of people who have been vaccinated.
24 あなたにまたお会いできる日を楽しみにしている．	I am looking forward to seeing you again.

【例文集2の解説】

1 Because people ① tend to get married later in life, the number of children that couples raise is becoming smaller than before.
【別解】Because ② there is a tendency to get married later in life, the number of children that couples raise is becoming smaller than before.
【解説】① tend to do … ＝…する傾向がある
② tendency を使った書き方もある．

2 We have to perform a lot of basic studies before we establish a new therapy.
【別解】It takes a lot of basic studies to establish a new treatment.
【解説】別解の「It takes O to do … ＝…するのに O を必要とする」をぜひ覚えてほしい．

3 It is becoming clear that many neurodegenerative diseases are caused by improper protein processing.
【解説】「It is clear that S V …」という形が元にある．

4 It is estimated that Japan's population will start decreasing in 2006. If this decrease continues, Japan's population will get half as large in 2100 as it is now.

〔語句〕半減する＝ decrease by half　　It is estimated that S V … ＝…と推定される

5　The reason why I left you for another man is that you are indecisive.
【解説】関係副詞の why を用いて理由を述べている．

6　①<u>A study shows that</u> this substance helps make blood pressure low.
【解説】①研究や調査やグラフからわかったことを述べる際に使える形．

7　<u>It was only in 2003 that</u> we finished sequencing the human genome.
【解説】強調構文である．

8　Compared with the previous data, this result is compatible / consistent with theoretical values.
〔参考〕the values（obtained）from theoretical calculations ＝理論計算の値
【解説】compared with … ＝…と比較して ⇒ 間違えて，「comparing with…」にしてはいけない．

9　Many diseases may be diagnosed based on a chest X-ray test.
【解説】based on … ＝…に基づいて ⇒ 前置詞のように使っていけばよい．

10　He teaches people with disabilities skills <u>they can use to earn a living</u>.
【解説】they の前に関係代名詞が省略されている．関係代名詞は正確に使えるようにしっかり訓練しておくこと．

〔参考〕関係代名詞の基礎
　　簡単な例文を使って関係代名詞の基礎を確認しておく．

例文１：The book which I bought yesterday is interesting.
　この例文での関係代名詞 which の働き
①先行詞である「the book」とは，世の中にいろいろある本のうちの「どれ」なのかということに関心を向ける．
② which 以降の文には，必ず穴が開いているよという合図になっている．その穴に先行詞である「the book」を代入すると，the book がどの本なのかがわかる仕組みになっている．
　例文１では，bought の後に穴が開いている（目的語が抜けている）ので，the book をそこに代入してやればどの本かがわかる．代入すると，I bought the book yesterday. となり，これを訳せば，the book とは，「私が昨日買った本」だということがわかる．

> 例文2：This is the child who surprised me.
> ⇒ surprised の S に穴が空いているので，そこに the child を代入すれば，the child が誰なのかがわかるようになっている．
>
> 例文3：He likes the movie which you talked about yesterday.（彼は，昨日あなたが話していた映画が好きだ）
> ⇒ which 以降を見ると，about の後ろに穴が空いている．よって，the movie をそこに代入すれば the movie がどの映画のことをいっているのかがわかる．
>
> 例文4：He likes the movie about which you talked yesterday.
> 【解説】例文3はこのように書き換えることができることも覚えておいてほしい．「前置詞＋関係代名詞」という形である．
>
> ・関係代名詞の省略
> 　例文1と例文3では，仮に関係代名詞が書かれていなくても，bought と about の後ろに穴が空いていることはかなりわかりやすい．よって，例文1（目的語に穴が空いている）や例文3（前置詞の後ろに穴が空いている）の場合には，関係代名詞を省略してもよい．例文2は，関係代名詞を省略すると，どこに穴が空いているのかがわかりにくくなるので省略できない．例文4の場合も省略はしない．

11　A pop quiz means a short test that a teacher gives without any warning, in order to check whether students have been studying.
【解説】check whether S V … ＝…かどうかを確かめる ⇒ とてもよく使う表現．

12　Whether we can master English depends on three factors.
【解説】「depend on … ＝…に左右される，…に依存している」の主語に，whether の節をもってくる形．

13　Whether women need an abortion is a controversial topic.
【解説】「議論の的」と出てきたらこの表現を使えばよい．

14　Anemia is a common blood disorder that occurs when there are fewer red blood cells than normal.
【解説】「通常よりも」「普通よりも」といいたければ，「than normal」が使える．

15　If the brain were so simple we could understand it, we would be so simple we couldn't.
【解説】仮定法過去の基本形．確実に使えないといけない．

16 If you had not called me, I would have overslept.
【解説】仮定法過去完了.

17 It is important not only to maintain adequate nutrient levels in the blood, but also to eliminate wastes and toxins.
〔語句〕not only A but also B ＝ A というだけでなく B も

18 Smartphones are essential to our daily life.
【解説】be essential to … ＝ …にとって必要不可欠な ⇒ よく使う.

19 Cats are different from dogs in the way they behave.
〔語句〕be different from A in B ＝ A と B の点で異なる

20 Medical professionals in the future will have to focus on lifestyle-related diseases.
〔語句〕focus on … ＝ …に焦点を当てる

21 The atomic nucleus is usually composed of one or more protons and some neutrons.
〔語句〕be composed of … ＝ …から成る

22 Japan depends on foreign countries for oil.
〔語句〕depend on A for B ＝ A に B を頼る

23 These days, people are rarely exposed to measles due to the high number of people who have been vaccinated.
〔語句〕be exposed to … ＝ …にさらされる

24 I am looking forward to seeing you again.
〔語句〕look forward to doing … ＝ …するのを楽しみしている

第2章
テーマ別問題演習

2.1 医師と患者の関係

p.30【問題11】 新潟大学 平成21年

問題の特徴

標準的なレベルの問題だと思われる．まずは問1, 問4の和訳問題で確実に点を取りたい．点を取れないとすると語彙力不足といえる．残りの内容説明問題も下線部の前後をしっかり見ていれば解答できるので，頑張ってほしい．

本文のテーマ

医師と患者のコミュニケーションの大切さについて論じた英文であるが，大きくいえば，医師と患者の関係というテーマといえる．医師と患者の関係に関する有名な資料として真っ先にあげられるのは「ヒポクラテスの誓い」であろう．これは医療者の心得を説いたものとして現在でも尊重されるべきものではあるが，医師と患者の関係をパターナリズム（ここでは素人である患者は専門家である医師の意見に従えばよいという姿勢のこと）の視点で捉えている点については，問題ありとされている．現在では，患者の自己決定権というものを基軸にして，医師と患者の関係を捉えなくてはいけないとされている．そして，この自己決定権を基軸とした医師・患者関係において重要な役割をはたしているのが，インフォームドコンセント（十分な説明を受けたうえでの同意）という考えだといえよう．こうした状況の下では，医師と患者の間で，良好で効果的なコミュニケーションが行われることが，治療を円滑に行っていくうえで必要不可欠となるであろう．

なお，本問以外にも医師と患者のコミュニケーションをテーマとする英文が出題された場合はある．たとえば，浜松医科大学や旭川医科大学で出題されたことがある．旭川医科大学では，自分の子供に予防接種を受けさせようとしない親と医師がどのようにコミュニケーションを取っていくべきかということを論じた英文が出題された．

解答

問1【解答例】 コミュニケーション能力の訓練が，患者の感情的苦痛と関連してくる医療過程や治療成果にどのような影響を与えているかについて探究した研究において，医師のコミュニケーション能力の改善は患者の精神的苦痛を軽減することにつながるということ

が証明された．

【解説】
a) In a study that explored ① the effects of communication-skills training on the process and outcome of care ② associated with patient's emotional distress, improvement in physicians' communication skills was shown to be associated with a reduction in emotional distress in patients.

　下線①は「the effect of A on B ＝ AのBに対する影響」という形になっている．この形はよく出てくる．「AがBにどんな影響を及ぼすか」という意訳ができることも覚えておいてほしい．また「be associated with … ＝ …と関連がある」という表現が2回出てきているので注意．これは必須熟語である．下線②は，be動詞が消えて，「associated with …」の部分だけで出てきている．これは過去分詞の形容詞用法である．このパターンは基本的な形なので，すぐに見抜けるようにしておきたい．

問2【解答例】患者本位のコミュニケーションがどの程度行われているかが，患者の不快感の軽減，不安感の軽減，精神衛生の向上と関係してくるという結果が出た．また，公的医療（サービス）の利用の減少との関連でいえば，自分たちが診察を受けに行った時に，それが患者本位であったと感じた患者はその後の数カ月で診断テストや専門医への照会が減ったという結果が出た．

【解説】
　以下に示した下線部b)の直後の箇所を訳せばよい．
the degree of patient-centred communication was associated with ① less discomfort, less concern and better mental health in patients. Moreover, ② in terms of reduction of utilisation of health services, it was shown that patients who perceived that their visits had been patient centred received fewer diagnostic tests and referrals in the subsequent months.

　下線①の訳し方に工夫が必要である．「より少ない不快感，より少ない不安感，よりよい精神衛生」という直訳は不自然である．ここは，【解答例】にあるように「不快感の軽減，不安感の軽減，精神衛生の向上」というふうに意訳できるとよい．
＊ポイント：「形容詞＋名詞」を訳す時には，名詞を訳してから形容詞を訳すという逆転の発想が役立つ時がしばしばある．上記の例でいえば，discomfortを訳してからlessを訳すということ．
下線②「in terms of … ＝ …との関連で」という熟語をしっかり覚えておいてほしい．

問3【解答例】患者の服薬遵守を向上させるうえで，医師と患者の関係が重要な役割をはたすということ．たとえば，医師の患者に対する態度や，患者が何に関心があるかを引き

出し，それを尊重する能力や，適切な情報の提供や，共感を示し患者の信頼を生み出すことが，治療法の遵守を高める際の重要な決定因子となることがわかっている．

【解説】
　まずは下線部の直前をしっかり理解することが大切である．
Finding ways to improve compliance is of interest to both health service administrators and physicians. To this end, c) <u>the doctor patient relationship may have an important role to play</u>.
→「to this end」は，「この目的を達成するために」という意味の重要な熟語である．ここでの「この目的」とは，直前の文を読めば，「服薬遵守を向上させるという目的」であることがわかる．この熟語をつけ加えて下線部 c) を訳すと，<u>an important role</u> がどのような役割かがわかってくると思う．後は下線部 c) の次の文の内容を解答に含めておけばよいであろう．

問4【解答例】患者の満足度は，我々の注目に値する重要な領域である．なぜならば，医療サービスに対する不満が生まれると，患者による医師への訴訟が起こったり，再三の診察により無駄な医療費の支出が生じてしまう．そしで両方とも医療制度にとって大きな損失になりうるだろう．

【解説】文法的にはとくに難しいところはない．単語力が重要となる．
〔語句〕　result in … = …をもたらす　　　litigation = 訴訟
　　　　 expenditure = 支出　　　　　　　 visit = 往診，診察，通院
　　　　 costly = 損失が大きい，費用がかかる

問5【解答例】医師が自らのプロとしての生き方に満足していると，患者のプライマリーケア医への信頼が高まるという効果がある．自分により満足している医師は，患者の不安により上手に対応できるようになるという効果もある．自らのプロとしての生き方に満足している医師は，より好ましい雰囲気を生み出すかもしれない．そして，それが患者とのコミュニケーションに影響し，さらには患者の満足度にも影響してくる．

【解説】
　下線部 e) の次の文の，以下の箇所を参考にすればよい．
In a study conducted in the outpatient division of a teaching hospital, it was shown ……… more positive effect, which may in turn affect their communication with patients which then affect patient satisfaction (Hall, 1988).

p.33 【問題 12】 東海大学医学部一般編入試験　平成 23 年

問題の特徴

東海大学の一般編入試験の英語でよく出題されるタイプの長文問題である．内容一致問題だけでなく，語彙を問う問題，指示語を問う問題も入ってくる．大学入試レベルの基本的な単語をしっかり理解していれば十分対応できる内容である．

本文のテーマ

HeLa 細胞の事例をもとに，ヒトから採取した組織を研究者が利用する際の問題点を論じている．

1　HeLa 細胞について

　HeLa 細胞とは，1951 年に，米国の Johns Hopkins 病院で子宮頸癌の治療を受けた Henrietta Lacks という黒人女性から採取された細胞である．この病院のある医師は，癌研究のために，体外においてヒトの細胞を継代培養していく方法を長年探していた．しかしその方法を見つけることはできていなかった．そんな時にこの医師は HeLa 細胞を見つけたのである．この細胞は不死化しており，体外でも細胞分裂を無制限にくり返した．この医師はただちに HeLa 細胞を仲間の研究者達に配りはじめ，やがてそれは全米に広まった．今では世界中でこの細胞が利用されている．

2　HeLa 細胞の功績

　Jonas Salk が最初のポリオワクチンをテストするために HeLa 細胞を使った．また，無重力状態がヒトの細胞に与える影響を調べるために月に持って行かれた．癌やエイズ，遺伝子診断の研究や，インフルエンザ，ヘルペス，パーキンソン病などの薬の研究のためにも使われている．

3　問題点

　HeLa 細胞を採取した医師は，Henrietta Lacks の同意や許可を取っていなかった．無断で採取し，無断で利用したということである．今ではこれはインフォームドコンセントの原理に反し，許されない行為であろう．しかし当時はまだこの原理がそこまで浸透していなかった．また，Johns Hopkins 病院の医師たちは，医療費を払えないような貧しい患者に医療を提供していたので，その代償として，患者を研究に利用してもよいだろうという考えを普通にもっていたのである．

4　現在におけるヒト由来物質の利用について

　ヒト由来物質の研究を行う際には，本人の同意が必要である．ヘルシンキ宣言の 1 条，25 条に規定されている．

ヘルシンキ宣言1条：The World Medical Association (WMA) has developed the Declaration of Helsinki as a statement of ethical principles for medical research involving human subjects, including research on identifiable human material and data. The Declaration is intended to be read as a whole and each of its constituent paragraphs should not be applied without consideration of all other relevant paragraphs.

〔和訳〕世界医師会（WMA）は，個人を特定できるヒト由来の試料およびデータに関する研究を含めた，人間を対象とする医学研究の倫理的原則として，ヘルシンキ宣言を発展させてきた．本宣言は，総合的に解釈されることを意図したものであり，（この宣言を構成している）各項目は他のすべての関連項目を考慮せずに適用されるべきではない．

ヘルシンキ宣言25条：For medical research ① using identifiable human material or data, physicians must normally seek consent for the collection, analysis, storage and/or reuse. There may be situations ② [where ③ consent would be impossible or impractical to obtain for such research ④ or would pose a threat to the validity of the research]. In such situations the research may be done ⑤ only after consideration and approval of a research ethics committee.

〔和訳〕個人を特定しうるヒト由来の試料またはデータを使用する医学研究に関しては，医師は収集，分析，保存および（または）再利用に対する同意を通常求めなければならない．このような研究には，同意を得ることが不可能であるか非現実的である場合，または研究の有効性に脅威を与える場合があり得る．このような状況下の研究は，研究倫理委員会の審議と承認を得た後にのみ行うことができる．

〔要点〕
① doing の形容詞用法．medical research を修飾している．
② 関係副詞の where が節をつくっている．先行詞は situations である．where 以下がどんな situations なのかを説明しているということになる．なお，situation(s) が先行詞の場合には，関係副詞の when をもってきてもよい．
　例文：There are situations when a doctor may decide to use a drug that is not specifically approved for children given the serious nature of the illness.
　（病気の重大性を考慮して，子供のために特別に認可されてはいない薬を使うことを医師が決断するかもしれないという状況がある）
③ 言い換えると，「It would be impossible or impractical to obtain consent for such research.」となる．「It is easy to answer the question. ＝ The answer is easy to answer.」と同じパターン．
④ この or により，「would be impossible or impractical」と「would pose a threat to the validity」が列挙されている．

⑤ only と時を表す言葉が使われると,「only ＝ようやく,はじめて」という訳が有効な場合が多い.ここでも,この訳を使ってもかまわない.
〔語句〕pose a threat to … ＝…に脅威をもたらす,…を脅かす
　　　　validity ＝正当性,妥当性

注1：ヘルシンキ宣言の和訳は,日本医師会が作成したものである.
注2：北海道大学と大阪大学では,ヘルシンキ宣言がそのまま試験で出題されたことがある.一度は全体に目を通しておきたい.

5　インフォームドコンセントについて
(1) 定義：患者が,現在の病状,検査や可能な治療方法とそのリスク,治療拒否の場合の予後などの十分な説明を医療者から受け,それを理解したうえで自分が受ける検査・治療を選択し,決定し（同意し）,あるいは拒否すること.

(2) 歴史的背景：アメリカの法廷で確立してきた概念である.
① 1914年　シュレンドルフ事件（同意の必要性）
　患者シュレンドルフは,ある検査を受けることには同意していたが,その後に手術を受けることまでは同意していなかった.しかし,医師は検査に続いて手術も行ってしまい,結果として,左足の指を数本切断するに至った.
⇒判決：同意なしに手術することは暴行に当たるとした.

② 1957年　サルゴ事件（同意のための十分な情報の必要性）
　マーティン・サルゴは,同意の上である検査を受けた.しかしその後,下半身が麻痺してしまった.医師からは事前に麻痺のリスクがあるという説明はなかった.説明しなかったことについて医師に過失があると訴えた.
⇒判決：同意に必要な情報として,治療の性格,予後,リスク,利益,代わりとなる治療などの情報を提供しないといけないとした.

まとめ：上記の2つの事件により,インフォームドコンセントという概念が確立された.

解答

(1)【解答例】イ

【解説】「unparalleled」は「比類なき」という意味である．これと同じ意味になるのは，イの「unprecedented（先例のない）」である．「precedent（先例）」という単語を知っていると覚えやすい．「unpredictable」は「予測不可の」という意味．

(2)【解答例】ア

【解説】確実に正解してほしい問題である．「immortal」は，「mortal」の反意語であり，「不死の」という意味である．普段から同意語や反意語を意識して単語を勉強してほしい．

(3)【解答例】エ

【解説】「the medical advances and industry profits (3) they generated ＝ それらが生み出してきた医学的な進歩や産業的な利益」という和訳ができれば，「they ＝ Lacks' prolific cells」ということが推測できる．theyの直前に関係代名詞thatが省略されている．

(4)【解答例】エ

【解説】エは，【3段落】の第1文と合致する．イはおかしい．これだと「無重力状態を経験するためにHeLa細胞を科学者達が使った」という意味になる．

(5)【解答例】ア

【解説】下線部 (5) の内容は直後の部分で具体化されている．
→「— scientists still haven't pinpointed why Lacks' cells are able to survive and thrive in the lab when others die off within months —」（科学者たちは，他の細胞は数ヶ月以内に死ぬのに，なぜLacksの細胞だけは，実験室で生存し，増殖できるのかをまだ正確に突き止めることはできていない）
　この部分の和訳ができれば，アが正解だとわかるであろう．

(6)【解答例】ウ

【解説】field ＝ answer, reply to

(7)【解答例】エ

【解説】crooked ＝不正直な，心の曲がった　　leading ＝主役の，すぐれた
　　　　reliable ＝信頼できる　　　　　　　　clear-headed ＝頭のさえた

(8)【解答例】イ

【解説】「institutionalized ＝施設に収容された」「sibling ＝兄弟」なので，【6段落】で述べられていた，Henrietta Lacks の第2子である Elsie Lacks を指すことがわかる．【6段落】を読むと，Elsie Lacks はてんかんのために，「Hospital for the Negro Insane」という病院で生活することになったという記述がある．

(9)【解答例】ウ

【解説】【7段落】の第1文で，Deborah は，母親のことだけでなく，妹に関する真実も知ろうとしたという指摘がなされている．そして第2文で Deborah の苦しい胸の内が明かされている．イの「be discouraged from doing …」は，「…しないように勧められる，…しないほうがよい」という意味．

(10)【解答例】ウ

【解説】
ア　【11段落】の内容に合致する．
イ　【12段落】の内容に合致する．
ウ　【10段落】の第1文に反する．after は，ここでは「ちなんで」という意味である．
エ　【11段落】の内容に合致する．

2.2 最新医療技術

p.37【問題13】 千葉大学 平成19年

問題の特徴

ヒトゲノムの解読という典型的なテーマなので，予備知識等をもっている人ならやりやすい問題であったと思われる．解答に必要な箇所も見つけやすいつくりになっている．専門的記述も含まれていて読みづらい部分もあるが，その部分は露骨に問われているわけではないので何とかなる．

ただし，設問で要求されている文字数と，英文の長さ，試験時間を比較してみると，かなりつらい問題である．時間内にどこまで答案を埋められるかが勝負である．似たような話題の英文を以前に読んだことがあれば，かなり有利になるであろう．

本文のテーマ

「1000ドルゲノムプロジェクト」とは，1人のゲノムの全塩基配列を1000ドルで決定できる技術を開発するという試みのこと．アメリカで盛んに行われている．本文でも，1000ドルという目標を達成するために，新しい技術開発が進められているということが述べられていた．

このプロジェクトの目的は，個人の体質に合った病気の予防法や治療法を開発するということにある．いわゆるオーダーメイド医療（personalized medicine，テーラーメイド医療ともいう）である．とくに，糖尿病や心筋梗塞などの生活習慣病の予知，予防が大きな目標となっている．個人のゲノムをすべて調べて，疾患のリスクを高めるSNP（1塩基多型）をすべてピックアップすることができれば，病気を予知，予防する際に役立つ．

もっとも，1000ドルゲノムプロジェクトには課題も残されている．1000ドルで究極の個人情報であるゲノム情報が得られるわけなので，濫用される危険性がある．濫用をどうやって防ぐのかという課題に真剣に取り組まないといけないであろう．

解答

問1 【解答例】 最初の段階では，ヒトゲノムのDNA構造の解読のために，1990年から2005年の間に30億ドルの費用がかけられた．この間の解読作業を通じて生まれてきた技術がその後，改良されていき，最近では，約2000万ドル程度で実用に耐えられる精度でのゲノム解読が可能になった．（131字）

【解説】

（1）については【1段落】の最終文を参照すればよい．（2）については【2段落】の第2文を参照すればよい．

問2 【解答例】一生に一度は，自分の全ゲノムを解読してもらうことが価値あることだと人々が思うかもしれないほど，DNAの塩基配列の解読費用が安価なものになるだろうという期待感を述べようとしている．こうなれば，研究者数や，病気の人と健康な人のゲノムの違いを理解するために比較可能なゲノム数も増える．また，病原体や体内の善玉菌やアレルゲンとなる生物のゲノム解析も進み，その結果を我々の日々の行動に生かせるかもしれない．また，有用な分子や汚染物質を分解するような微生物を見つけることもできるかもしれない．（240字）

【解説】
　まずは，【3段落】の第1文のthe promise以降がポイントになる．後は，【3段落】の第2文と【4段落】をまとめることになる．
〔語句〕be shorthand for … ＝…の別の言い方である，…の言い換えである
〔英文解説〕
The "$1,000 genome" has become shorthand for the promise of DNA-sequencing capability ① made so affordable that individuals might think the once-in-a-lifetime expenditure to have a full personal genome sequence read to a disk for doctors to reference is worthwhile.
和訳：1000ドルゲノムとは，次のような期待を簡明に表現するための言葉になった．その期待とは，自分のゲノムの完全な塩基配列を，医師が参照できるようにディスクに読み取ってもらうために，一生に一度くらいはお金を出すことが，価値のあることだと思えるかもしれないほどに，DNAの塩基配列を解読するための技能が手頃なものになるだろうというものだ．
⇒① made以下は，過去分詞が導く長い語群となっており，直前のcapabilityに説明を加えている．ここでは，madeの後に，affordableという形容詞がきている．この形を訳す時には，次のような，同じ形（made＋形容詞）を含んだ受動態の文を思い浮かべること．
例文：I am made happy by her smile.（私は，彼女の笑顔によって幸せな気持ちにさせられる→私は彼女の笑顔によって幸せな気持ちになる）
　この例文を見ると，「made happy（made＋形容詞）」という部分を，「幸せな気持ちになる（形容詞の状態になる）」と訳している．この訳し方を本問でも使えばよい．
　よって本問では，affordableの前にsoが入っているので，それを含めて訳すと，「made so affordable＝それほど手頃な状態になる」となる．つまり直前の「DNA-sequencing capability」が「それほど手頃な価格になる」と説明している．
　さらにここではもう一つ問題がある．それは，「それほど（so）」とは，「どれほどか」ということである．これを説明をしているのが，後ろにくるthat節である．このようにsoの内容をthat節で説明するというのは，英語でよく出てくる形だった．この形のせいで，本問ではmade以下が非常に長くなっている．
　「have a full personal genome sequence read to a disk for doctors to reference」も

難しい．read は過去分詞で，「have O done」という形になっている．直訳すると，「自分のゲノムの塩基配列が，ディスクに読み取られるという状態をもつ」となる．意訳すると，「自分のゲノムの塩基配列を，ディスクに読み取ってもらう」くらいになる．

　ここでは，made と read はともに過去分詞である．過去分詞は，直前に have（または has）や be 動詞がついていれば処理しやすいが，それらがついていない場合には，処理しづらくなるので注意．

問 3　【解答例】2009 年までに 10 万ドルの費用で，そして，2014 年までには 1000 ドルの費用で，1 人分のヒトゲノムを解読できるようにするということを目的としているプログラム．また，最初にこの偉業をなしとげた研究チームには，賞金が与えられることになっている．(122 字)

【解説】下線部 (2) の直後と，その次の文を読めば解答できる．
〔語句〕challenge O to do … ＝ O に…する気を起こさせる

問 4　【解答例】最も費用がかかるのは試薬と装置である．費用を下げるために装置の小型化が行われた．これにより，試薬の使用量を，従来のサンガー法に比べて 10 億分の 1 に減らすことができた．具体的にいえば，試薬使用量の単位がマイクロリットルからフェムトリットルにまで下がった．(126 字)

【解説】【9 段落】の第 3 文，第 4 文がポイントになる．問 4 の設問文を見れば，この 2 つの文を意識して設問をつくっていることがわかるであろう．
〔語句〕reagent ＝試薬

問 5　【解答例】今日米国や日本などで生まれるすべての赤ん坊は，出生後退院する前に必ずフェニルケトン尿症という遺伝病の検査を受ける．ある種の肺ガン患者では，イレッサという抗ガン剤の効き目を調べるために，EGFR という遺伝子の変異を調べる．イレッサ以外の薬でも，投与量を決める際に，患者がそれをどのように代謝するかを調べるために遺伝子検査が行われる．安価に個人のゲノムが調べられるようになることで，こうしたオーダーメイド医療が可能となる．また，医療応用のほかに系統学的研究にも利用できる．私たちの顔や姿，気質は，遺伝子どうし，あるいは遺伝子と環境とのどのような相互作用によって形づくられるのかを解明していくこともできる．(300 字)

【解説】
　最後の 2 つの段落をじっくり読んでまとめればよい．最終段落の最終文には，「make it possible to do…＝ …することを可能にする」という基本構文が出てきている．it が形式目的語で真目的語が「to do…」となっている．

〔語句〕 see if SV… = …かどうかを確かめる　　be likely to do… = …する可能性がある
　　　　dosage = 服用量　　　　　　　　　　　trait = 特徴，形質
　　　　comprise = 構成する，形作る　　　　　 unravel = 解明する

問6　【解答例】 ①科学者や保険会社，雇用主，裁判所，学校，養子縁組斡旋業者，行政機関，さらには医療関係者や子供を望むカップルなどが，個人の遺伝情報を使用するにあたり，プライバシーや公平性をどのようにして保証すればよいのかという問題が生じる．この点がうまく解決されなければ，遺伝情報による差別が生じる．また，②仮に，プライバシーや公平性が担保されたとしても，入手した遺伝情報を本人が正確に理解し，うまく利用できるような社会的土壌が整っていないという問題が残る．また，すべての医師が，患者の遺伝情報をどんなアドバイスをすべきかという点において，十分な教育を受けているとは限らないという点も問題となる．(290字)

【解説】
　この問題は，「本文の内容をふまえつつ，自分の考えを書く」というものである．こうした問題では，当たり前ではあるが，「本文の内容をふまえつつ」という点を一番大切にしてほしい．「自分の考え」として何を書くかは，本文の内容次第となる．自分の考えなら何でも書いてよいというわけではない．「自分の考えを」という言葉に引きずられて，小論文的な問題と捉えるのはあまりよくない．あくまでも内容理解を問う問題であるという姿勢の方がよい．
　下線部①は，本文の【12段落】の最終文（But many of the really big questions remain…）をふまえての解答である．下線部②では，下線部①の内容をふまえつつ，本文では指摘されていない重要な問題点を指摘した．本文では，遺伝情報を入手した個人や，その個人から相談を受ける可能性がある医師が遺伝情報を適切に処理できるかという点に関してはほとんど指摘されていない．

p.42【問題14】 千葉大学 平成23年

問題の特徴

　ES 細胞や iPS 細胞やクローン技術などが出てくる問題．非常に有名な論点が出てくるので，しっかりと得点したい問題である．英語の力に加えて，予備知識も非常に大切であり，総合力が問われるであろう．なお，常日頃から，このような典型論点を含む英文には必ず目を通すようにし，試験で出題された場合には得点源にしてほしい．

本文のテーマ

　ES 細胞と iPS 細胞が登場する．両者とも，ヒトの体を構成しているあらゆる細胞に分化する能力をもった特殊な幹細胞であるという点では共通しているが，作成法に大きな違いがあるので確認しておく必要がある．

表　ES 細胞と iPS 細胞

幹細胞の種類	作成法	特徴
通常の ES 細胞	胚盤胞（受精卵ができてから5～6日後の状態）の中にある内部細胞塊を取り出して特定の条件で培養する．	・生命の萌芽である胚を破壊することになるので問題がある． ・この ES 細胞由来の細胞を治療のために患者に移植する場合に，拒絶反応の問題が生じる．患者の遺伝子と元になった受精卵の遺伝子は異なるからである．しかし，下記の2つの場合では，患者の体細胞を使えばこの問題を回避できる．
クローン胚由来の ES 細胞	ある人の体細胞の核を，除核済みの卵細胞に移植し，クローン胚をつくる．クローン胚の中にできる内部細胞塊を取り出して，培養する．	・卵細胞を確保するために，女性に卵細胞の提供を求めることになる． ・クローン胚をつくることはクローン人間の作成につながるかもしれず，問題がある．
iPS 細胞	ある人の体細胞に特定の遺伝子を導入し，ES 細胞と同じ条件で培養する．	・体細胞と特定の遺伝子さえあれば，ES 細胞と同じ能力をもった細胞がつくれる． ・上記の2つよりも簡単につくれるので，濫用される危険性が大きい．

iPS 細胞の利用法

(1) 細胞移植医療に使えるが，まだまだ克服しなくてはいけない問題はたくさんある．
例：パーキンソン病の治療
→運動器系の機能が損なわれる病気．ドーパミン分泌細胞の変性がこの病気の主な原因で

ある．そこで，iPS 細胞からドーパミン分泌細胞をつくり出し，移植することで治療できる可能性がある．

(2) 病気の原因やメカニズムを探る

　病気の原因やメカニズムを知るには，最終的に，その病気になっている人の細胞をたくさん確保して調べなければいけない．病気になっている人の細胞からいったん iPS 細胞を樹立できれば，細胞の安定供給が保証され，調べやすくなる．また，この iPS 細胞を病気と関わっている重要な細胞に分化させることで，その分化過程に何か異常がないかも調べられる．

(3) 医薬品開発のスクリーニング

　開発中の医薬品の効果をヒト iPS 細胞由来の細胞を使って調べられると，医薬品開発にとても役立つ．

解答
問 1【解答例】
(1a) give rise to → produce　　　　　(1b) flesh → tissue
(1c) coax → nudge または induce

【解説】
(1a)「give rise to … =…をもたらす」という熟語は必須である．ここでは「生み出す」という感じなので，produce でよいであろう．
(1b)「two quick nips of flesh」は，直前の「punch biopsy（パンチ生検）」の説明部分である．生検とは，そもそも組織を採取することであり，ここも「two quick nips of tissue（組織をすばやく 2 回挟み取ること）」と考えるのが自然であろう．
(1c) coax は，本文では，「導く」「誘導する」という意味で使われているが，この単語は本来は「説得する」という意味である．その点を考慮すると，nudge（【6 段落】の第 1 文参照）が一番意味が近い．nudge も説得するという意味だが，本文では，「導く」という意味で使われている．induce でも正解となるであろう．

問 2 【解答例】
(2a) 世界に衝撃を与えた．　　(2b) その考えを温めていた．　　(2c) 開始していた

【解説】
　単語力を問う問題である．前後関係から意味を推測する力も必要であろう．
〔語句〕electrify ＝衝撃を与える　　　　　　nurse ＝大事にはぐくむ，心に抱く
　　　　embark on … =…をはじめる

問3 【解答例】

3a → to   3b → In   3c → for   3d → by

【解説】

3a　extent は，to と仲がよい．　cf. to some extent ＝ある程度まで

3b　「in response ＝それに応じて」という熟語．文頭にくる場合が多く，直前の文の内容を受けて使われる．

3c　promise を「見込み」「期待」という意味で使う場合には，前置詞 for と馴染む．cf. The stem cell research may hold promise for treating Alzheimer's disease.（その幹細胞研究により，アルツハイマー病が治療できるという期待がもてるかもしれない）

3d　「by doing … ＝…することによって」という形になる．

問4 【解答例】without needing to use or destroy an embryo

【解説】

ES 細胞の作製には胚の破壊を伴うが，iPS 細胞の作製の際には胚の破壊が伴わないという基本的知識があれば解答しやすい．

問5 【解答例】4

【解説】

not least は because の節などの前に置かれて，「特に」という意味で使われる．

問6 【解答例】培養皿の中で ALS を再現するという考えを実現するのに必要なもののうちで，iPS 細胞以外のもののことを指している．具体的には，クロアチアの姉妹や他の ALS 患者の細胞や，それらの細胞を備蓄しておくための研究所のこと．（106字）

【解説】

下線（6）のすぐ後に出てくる「in place」は大切な熟語である．ここでは「準備が整っている」という意味で使われている．よって下線（6）を含む文は，「培養皿の中で病気をつくり出すという考えを試すために必要な他のあらゆるものは，すでに準備が整っていた」という意味になる．そして次の文を見ると，「for example」とあるので，「必要な他のあらゆるもの」の具体例が出てくることがわかる．ここまで見えれば解答のメドが立つ．

問7 【解答例】A29 と呼ばれる患者はかなり長い間 ALS にかかっており，その程度も重かった．この人から iPS 細胞を樹立できたことで，iPS 細胞の手法を，重大で一生続く疾患を反映した細胞をつくるために使える可能性があるということが実証された．（112字）

【解説】
【11段落】の第2文の「the age and degree of illness in patient A29 demonstrated that the iPS technique could be used to create cells that reflected a serious, lifelong disease.」という箇所がポイントになる．第4文（We wanted to prove the point that you could reprogram cells even from a very, very, very, very old person who'd been sick for some length of time.）も参考になる．
〔語句〕headliner ＝立役者

問8 【解答例】従来の科学者は，幹細胞から分化した細胞を導き，その細胞を疾患をもつ患者に移植して病気を治すということに焦点を当てていたが，ルービンは，幹細胞を利用して，培養皿の中で病気を再現し，それをもとに薬を発見しようとしていた．（108字）

【解説】
【6段落】の第2文以降（とくに第4文）と【7段落】の第1文がポイントになる．
【7段落】の第1文に出てくる「cell therapy」については【5段落】で説明されているので，そちらにも目を通す必要がある．

問9 【解答例】ES細胞を採取するには，ヒトの胚を破壊しなければならないので，道徳的な問題が提起された．ES細胞から分化した細胞をつくり出して移植するという療法をやろうにも，動物実験では失敗がくり返された．（95字）

【解説】
【4段落】の第1文と第2文，そして【5段落】の第1文を見れば，解答に必要な箇所がわかる．確実に解答したい問題である．具体的には，【4段落】の第2文のbecause節の部分と，【5段落】の最後から2つの文がポイントになる．

問10 【解答例】ドリーをつくったのと同じ技術を応用しようとしていた．エガンは，皮膚の細胞のような成熟細胞から核を採取し，それを除核された未受精卵に移植して胚のような細胞をつくろうとした．（85字）

【解説】
【9段落】の「He was trying to make embryolike cells the "old-fashioned" way, however, ☐3d☐ applying the same cloning technique that produced Dolly the sheep. Eggan would take the nucleus out of an adult cell, such as a skin cell, and implant it into an unfertilized egg whose own nucleus had been removed.」を訳せば解答できる．なお，「Dolly」とは1996年に生まれた世界初の体細胞クローンヒツジの名前である．

2.3 現代において問題となっている疾患

p.47【問題15】 愛媛大学 平成21年

問題の特徴

遺伝病に関する基本的な知識があれば非常に解きやすい問題である．英語の力も重要であるが，多少知らない単語があっても，遺伝病に関する知識で常識的な解答を導き出してほしい問題である．愛媛大学は読解問題が2～3題出題されるが，このような解きやすい問題から確実に解いていってほしい．

本文のテーマ

遺伝性疾患が本文のテーマとなっている．遺伝性疾患とは遺伝子の変化が原因となって生じる疾患で，現在1万種類以上が知られている．染色体異常症，単一遺伝子疾患，多因子遺伝病の3つに分類できる．

1 染色体異常症

染色体に数的異常や構造的異常が生じることで発生する病気．

〈代表例〉

(1) ダウン症：21番染色体が3本になっている．（数的異常）
(2) クラインフェルター症候群：男性に見られる病気で，性染色体に数的異常が生じている．具体的には，性染色体が「XXY」となっている場合があげられる．（数的異常）
(3) 網膜芽細胞腫：13番染色体の長腕が欠失している．（構造的異常）
(4) 慢性骨髄性白血病：染色体の転座により生じる病気．（構造的異常）

2 単一遺伝子疾患

単一の遺伝子の変異により生じるもので，メンデルの遺伝の法則に従って遺伝する．さらに遺伝形式により，常染色体優性遺伝病，常染色体劣性遺伝病，伴性遺伝病の3つに分類できる．

単一遺伝子疾患の代表例

常染色体優性遺伝病	常染色体劣性遺伝病	伴性遺伝病
ハンチントン病	鎌状赤血球貧血症（sickle cell anemia） 嚢胞性線維症（cystic fibrosis）	血友病（hemophilia） デュシェンヌ型筋ジストロフィー

3 多因子遺伝病
　複数の遺伝子や環境因子が関与して発症する病気．癌，糖尿病，虚血性心疾患，高脂血症などが代表例である．

〔参考〕上記の3つ以外に，「ミトコンドリア遺伝病」もある．これはミトコンドリアDNAの変異による疾患を指す．この変異により，ミトコンドリアの働きが低下すると，当然，細胞の活動も低下する．これにより，とくに筋肉の細胞や脳の神経細胞が影響を受けることになる．

解答
問1　下線(1)【解答例】 ほぼあらゆる疾患は，遺伝子と環境の作用が合わさった結果として生じるものだ．しかし，遺伝的要素の相対的な役割は，大きくなるかもしれないし，小さくなるかもしれない．（80字）

【解説】
　文構造は難しくない．内容を理解したうえで，いかに自然な日本語に意訳できるかがポイントになる．医学部学士試験の下線部和訳は，こうしたタイプの問題がけっこう多い．下線部分は，「合わさった作用」ではなく，「作用が合わさる」というふうに逆転させて訳せると自然な日本語になる．

下線(2)【解答例】 染色体異常において見られる欠陥は，遺伝情報に1つの誤りがあることで生じるのではない．染色体全体，または，染色体の一部分に含まれている遺伝子が多すぎたり，欠損していることで生じるのだ．（91字）

【解説】
「due not to A but to B＝AではなくBによるものだ」という形に注目してほしい．「contained in whole chromosomes or chromosome segments.」の部分は，直前のthe genes を修飾している．「excess（過剰）」「deficiency（欠失，欠損）」は必須単語である．「segment（部分，断片）」も覚えること．
〔語句〕genetic blueprint ＝遺伝情報

問2　【解答例】 単一遺伝子疾患は，単一遺伝子の変異によって生じる．単一遺伝子疾患には，普通，明白で特徴的な系統パターンが見られる．単一遺伝子疾患の頻度は，個別に見れば低いけれども，全部合わせると，病因や死因に占める割合はかなり大きい．（109字）

【解説】
【3段落】の第4文までは，いろいろ述べられているが，結局，第1文で述べられていること以上のことはいっていない．第5文は，単一遺伝子疾患の特徴的なパターンについて

述べられている．第4文までとは違う話題が出てきているので，要約に入れておく必要がある．第6文以降は単一遺伝子疾患の頻度の話をしている．第7文で述べられていることがポイントになるので，そこを要約に入れておけばよいであろう．第8文や第9文は第7文の具体例と見ればよく，要約に入れる必要はない．

問3　【解答例】 Multifactorial

【解説】
　multifactorialとは，「多因子の」という意味である．
【1段落】の最終文と，【2段落】【3段落】のはじまり方をチェックすれば，解答を導き出せる．

問4　【解答例】 遺伝病の種類と特徴と発生頻度について

【解説】
　遺伝病の種類が述べられていることは明らかである．また，【2段落】〜【4段落】を読むと，それぞれの遺伝病の特徴と頻度が説明されていることがわかる．

p.49【問題16】 愛媛大学　平成23年

問題の特徴

専門的な単語がそれなりに出てくる．遺伝学の知識があるとかなり解きやすい問題である．もっとも，下線部の周辺を見れば解答できるようになっており，答案をつくるだけであれば，それほど深い理解がなくとも何とかなるであろう．

本文のテーマ

2型糖尿病に関与している遺伝子の発見に関する文章である．まず糖尿病の説明をし，その後，疾患遺伝子を突き止める方法について説明する．

1　糖尿病

(1) 1型糖尿病

インスリンをつくっている膵臓のβ細胞が，自己免疫反応によって破壊されてしまうのが1型糖尿病である．体内のインスリン量が極端に減少してしまうので，インスリン注射が必要である．遺伝的に発病しやすい素因があり，それに何らかの環境的要因が加わり発症する．発病は10歳代がほとんどである．

(2) 2型糖尿病

インスリンの中程度の不足やインスリンの働きが悪くなることで生じるのが2型糖尿病である．普段，我々が糖尿病といっているのはこの2型糖尿病のことである．肥満や運動不足，栄養過剰等が重なって生じる生活習慣病である．発病は40歳代以降が普通．

2　疾患遺伝子を発見する方法

(1) linkage analysis（連鎖解析）

ある病気の患者とその家系に属する人々の血液サンプル等を集めてきて，ゲノム上の塩基配列の個人差をマーカーにする．そして，病気が家系内に伝わっていくパターンと，そのマーカーが家系内で伝わっていくパターンを比較し，疾患遺伝子の位置を突き止めていく方法である．

連鎖解析自体は，1900年代のはじめに遺伝学者モーガンによって確立された手法である．モーガンは，ショウジョウバエの遺伝子を調べるためにこの手法を使っていたにすぎず，ヒトにこの手法を適用するのは難しいとされていた．しかし，ヒトゲノム解析が進むにつれて，ゲノムの塩基配列中にはたくさんの個人差が見られることがわかってきた．この個人差を利用することで，連鎖解析がヒトにも適用できるようになった．これまでに，連鎖解析の利用により1500種類以上の遺伝病の原因となる遺伝子が発見されてきた．ハンチントン病遺伝子もそのうちの1つである．

(2) association analysis（関連解析，相関解析）
　ある大きな集団から，特定の病気にかかっている患者集団とそうでない正常集団を抽出してそのゲノムを比較することで，疾患関連遺伝子を突き止める方法のことである．複数の遺伝子やいろいろな環境要因によって生じる多因子疾患（癌，糖尿病，高血圧，アレルギー等）に関与している遺伝子の発見によく使われる．

解答
問1【解答例】
- family-based linkage analyses and focused candidate-gene studies（【1段落】の第2文）
- a switch to tests of association（【2段落】の第1文）
- systematic, large-scale surveys of association between common DNA sequence variants and disease（【3段落】の第1文）

問2【解答例】 association analysis

【解説】
　副詞節中の「Sとbe動詞」が省略される形が出てきている．このパターンは，副詞節中のSと主節のSが一致している場合にだけ生じる．とてもよく出てくる形なので，しっかり理解しておいてほしい．
　この問題は文法問題的な色彩が強い．学士試験では，やや珍しいタイプの問題である．なお，下線部の箇所を省略せずに書くと，以下のようになる．
⇒ Although association analysis（副詞節中のS）is <u>intrinsically more powerful</u> than linkage analysis, association analysis（主節のS）suffers from the disadvantage that the signal can be detected only if one examines the causal variant itself or a nearby marker with which it is tightly correlated.
〔参考〕副詞節中の「S＋be動詞」の省略
次の例文が典型例である．理解の助けに使ってほしい．
　You must be careful while driving a car.（whileの後に「you are」が省略されている）

問3【解答例】 ゆえに，関連性を全ゲノムレベルで調べることを可能にする手法が出現するまでは，研究者達は，候補となっている特定の変異や関心のある特定の遺伝子だけに，注意を向けざるを得なかった．

【解説】
　文構造を把握するのはそんなに難しくはない．単語力が重要となる．
〔語句〕advent ＝到来，出現　　　　be obliged to do … ＝…せざるを得ない

　　　　　of interest ＝関心のある

〔参考〕genome-wide association study（ゲノムワイド関連研究）

　病気に罹患している集団と一般対照集団との間で遺伝情報（アレルの出現頻度など）の違いを検定し，病気の原因となる遺伝子や多型を見出すという作業を，全ゲノム領域の各多型に対し行う方法．たとえば，糖尿病の関連遺伝子を見つけるには，糖尿病患者とそうでない人，それぞれ数千人の集団を対象に，ゲノム全域にわたって多型を比較する必要がある．

問 4　【解答例】約 40

【解説】
【4 段落】の「The current total of approximately 40 confirmed type 2 diabetes loci includes variants in or near *WFS1*（wolframin）and the hepatocyte nuclear factors *HNF1A* and *HNF1B*（genes that also harbor rare mutations responsible for monogenic forms of diabetes）」をふまえればよい．

問 5　【解答例】インスリンの分泌よりもむしろ，インスリンの作用に対して主たる影響を及ぼしている 2 型糖尿病の遺伝子座であるということ．（58 字）

【解説】下線部の直後を訳せれば解答できる．
〔参考〕*IRS1* について
　インスリンは，標的細胞の受容体に結合してはじめてその作用を発揮する．糖尿病の中にはこの受容体遺伝子に異常があるために正常な受容体が形成されず，糖尿病状態となるものがある（もっとも，このようなタイプの糖尿病は非常にまれであると考えられている）．
　インスリンが受容体に結合すると細胞内のインスリン受容体基質（IRS）といわれるタンパク質がリン酸化され，このあと次々と情報伝達が起こり最終的に血糖値が下がる方向に進む．
　この IRS は少なくとも 4 種類が知られており，それぞれ，IRS1, IRS2, IRS3, IRS4 と命名されている．
　このうち，IRS1 をつくらせる遺伝子の異常が糖尿病状態と関係のあることは比較的古くから知られていた．日本人の糖尿病の約 4 分の 1 にはこのタンパクの異常が認められるという報告がある．しかし，IRS1 に異常があっても IRS2 がこの働きを代償することがわかっており，IRS1 の異常のみでは糖尿病にはならない．さらに別の要素が加わって糖尿病が発病するものと考えられている．

p.52 【問題17】新潟大学　平成21年

問題の特徴

　各段落の内容をしっかり捉えつつ，下線部の前後を見ていけば，解答しやすい問題となっている．答案をつくる際にふまえなくてはいけない箇所に重要な構文や単語がたくさん含まれているので，しっかりと解答できてほしい問題である．

本文のテーマ

　胎生期の低栄養環境が，成人期の生活習慣病の発症に影響を及ぼすという考えが本文のテーマである．本文中に出てきている thrifty phenotype hypothesis（倹約表現型仮説）が特に重要である．

　これは，胎生期に低栄養環境に曝された成人は，少ないエネルギーを有効に利用すべく形質転換されており，出生後の将来の飢餓状態に適応しているという考え方である．しかしこのような省エネルギー体質は，現代のような飽食の時代においては不利に働くことになる．脂肪を蓄積しやすくなったり，耐糖能（上昇した血糖値を正常に戻す能力）の低下を来しやすいなどの適応不全を来し，結果としてメタボリックシンドローム発症のハイリスク群となってしまう可能性がある．

〔参考〕省エネルギー体質に関する遺伝子

　脂肪細胞に存在する $β_3$ アドレナリン受容体はアドレナリンに反応して脂肪を分解する役割を担っている．この受容体の遺伝子には多型が見られる．ある多型をもつ人だと，アドレナリンにまったく反応せず，脂肪の分解が進まない．こういう人は，体内に効率よく脂肪を蓄えることができるので，省エネルギー体質といえる．これは，低栄養環境では有利だが，飽食の時代においては肥満になりやすいということになる．なお，上記の $β_3$ アドレナリン受容体の遺伝子のように，エネルギーの倹約に関与している遺伝子は，「倹約遺伝子（thrifty gene）」と呼ばれることがある．

解答

(1)【解答例】 1911～1930年の間に，England南部のHertfordshire州で生まれた5600人以上の男性の運命を分析した結果，出生時や1歳時にもっとも体重が少なかった人々は，その後，虚血性心疾患による死亡率が最も高くなったということがわかった．また，死亡するリスクは，体重が軽い赤ちゃんのほうが，重い赤ちゃんよりもほぼ3倍高かったということがわかった．

【解説】

【1段落】の第4文以降に着眼すればよい．

〔語句〕go on to do … ＝続いて…する，次に…する　cf. go on doing … ＝…し続ける

(2)【解答例】赤ちゃんの頃に，これらの人々の誰もが痩せていなかったならば，後の冠動脈性心疾患の発生量は半分になっていたであろう．半分になるということは，公衆衛生の点で，非常に大きな潜在的利益となる．

【解説】
b) ① <u>had none of these people been thin as babies, then there would have been half as much coronary heart disease later</u> － ② <u>a huge potential gain in public health.</u>

下線①は，仮定法でよく見られる，「倒置による if の省略」というパターンである．普通に書くなら，「if none of these people had been thin as babies, …」となる．この if 節内を倒置させることで（ここでは疑問文の語順にするということ），if をカットできる．このパターンは，試験で問われることがしばしばあるので注意しておくこと．得点できれば，他の人に大きな差をつけられると思う．

下線②は，直前で述べた内容，すなわち，「後の冠動脈性心疾患の発生量は半分になっていた」ということを，別の言い方で表現し直している部分．文脈や常識から判断してほしい．こういう言い換えも英語ではよく出てくる．

(3)【解答例1】栄養状態が悪い赤ちゃんの体というのは，出生前の経験が刻み込まれており，一生の間，食べ物が欠乏した状態になるという予測のもとで生まれてくることになる．そうすると，赤ちゃんの代謝作用は調節されて，小さいことや，カロリーを蓄えること，過剰な運動を避けることにふさわしい状態になっていく．しかし，赤ちゃんが，食糧が豊富な時代にいることに気づくと，成長スピードを速めることで埋め合わせをする．しかし，その埋め合わせは，心臓に負担がかかるような形で行われることになる．

【解答例2】出生前の飢餓状態という環境に適合しようとした結果として，心臓病になってしまうという仮説である．出生前に飢餓状態にさらされた結果として，エネルギー倹約型の小さい体で生まれてきた赤ちゃんは，出生後，食糧が豊富な状態に置かれると，成長スピードを速めることで埋め合わせをする．しかし，その埋め合わせは，心臓に負担がかかるような形で行われることになり，心臓病になりやすくなる．

【解説】
【3段落】の第4文以降を理解できていれば解答できる．第4文以降をひたすら和訳してシンプルにつくったのが【解答例1】である．【解答例2】は，第4文以降の趣旨を捉えて自分の言葉で説明している感じである．【解答例2】のほうがわかりやすくまとまっているが，時間がないときは【解答例1】のような露骨な解答のほうが楽であり，実戦的かもしれない．

〔語句〕hoarding ＝貯蔵，蓄積　　　　　　　in a time of plenty ＝豊かな時代に
　　　　put a strain on … ＝…に負担をかける
〔参考〕【3段落】の最終文に出てくる「such a way as to put …」について

「such A as to do …」という形は，普通は「…するほどの A」と訳すことが多い．しかし，ここでは「…するような A」と訳したほうがよい．

(4)【解答例】 妊娠の最後の 3 ヶ月間に飢餓にさらされていた赤ちゃんは，出生時に低体重になってしまうという影響が出た．また，これらの赤ちゃんは普通に成長したが，後で，糖尿病にかかってしまうという影響も見られた．妊娠してから 6 ヶ月以内の時期に飢餓にさらされていた赤ちゃんは，通常の体重で生まれてきたが，その子たちが大人になった時にとても小さい赤ちゃんを出産するという影響も見られた．

【解説】
　下線部 d）だけでなく，それを含む文全体をしっかり理解して解答することが大切である．【5 段落】の最後から 2 つ目の文以降と【6 段落】の第 1 文がポイントになるであろう．なお，【5 段落】の最後から 3 つ目の文は，医学研究者の注意を引くような影響ではなく，一般的な影響を述べているだけなので，解答に入れなくてよいであろう．
〔語句〕gestation ＝妊娠

(5)【解答例】 人の場合，倹約的な表現型と贅沢型の表現型の切り換えに数世代かかるため，France 政府は，1870 年代の独仏戦争の後から妊婦への配給を増強しはじめたので，現代ではこの切り換えが済んでいるが，Finland の人々は 50 年前までは，比較的貧困な状態で暮らしていたため，まだこの切り換えが完成していないと考えられる．よって，心疾患の死亡率が France の 4 倍になっている．

【解説】
　下線部 e）を含む文をしっかり理解することが大切である．
If it takes several generations for humans to switch between thrifty and affluent phenotypes, ① this may explain why e) Finland has nearly four times the death rate from heart disease as in France.
　下線①に注目してほしい．「this may explain why …」となっている．これを直訳すると，「これが，なぜ…なのかを説明しているかもしれない」となる．この直訳から，why 以下の理由が，「this」であることがわかる．よって，下線部 e）の理由は this ということになる．ここでは，this は直前にある if 節の内容を指している．if 節内には，「it takes O for ～ to do … ＝～が…するのに O を必要とする」という構文が出てきている．this の中身を答案化した後に，下線部 e）の直後にくる 3 文の内容に言及しておくとよりわかりやすい答案になる．

p.55【問題18】 高知大学 平成21年

問題の特徴
　アルツハイマー病の知識があれば解きやすい問題となっている．ただし，知識に頼りすぎてはいけない．英語の問題なので，最終的には本文の記述をきちんと確認して解かないといけない．ほぼすべての段落に目を通さないと解けない問題となっている．どの段落に何が書いてあるかを短時間でつかめるように頑張ってほしい．なお，基本的なことだが，先に設問を見て文の概容を把握しようとすることも重要である．こうした選択式の問題の場合には，この作業を忘れないでほしい．

本文のテーマ
　アルツハイマー病がテーマとなっている．アルツハイマー病は進行性の認知力低下を引き起こす病気で，現代では，最も一般的な認知症の原因となっている．

アルツハイマー病の特徴
　老人斑，神経原線維変化，神経細胞の脱落による脳の萎縮という3つの病理学的特徴が脳に見られる．
　老人斑とは，簡単にいうとタンパク質のかすが脳の神経細胞の周りに沈着したもので，その主成分はβアミロイドタンパク質と呼ばれるものである．このβアミロイドには神経毒性があり，アルツハイマー病の原因物質ではないかと考えられている．老人斑は，アルツハイマー病の人の脳以外だと，ダウン症の人の脳でしか見られない．よって老人斑はとても特徴的な現象といえる．
　神経原線維変化とは，簡単にいうと古くなった繊維状のタンパク質が掃除されずに細胞内に溜まって"ゴミ"のようになってしまう現象のことである．この現象はアルツハイマー病以外の病気でも見られるので，アルツハイマー病に特異的な現象ではない．
　神経細胞の脱落による脳の萎縮というのも有名な特徴である．もっとも進んだ場合だと，正常な場合の60％くらいにまで萎縮していることがある．とくに大脳新皮質の記憶や思考に関与している部分や，記憶に重要な海馬周辺で，神経細胞の脱落が顕著に見られるということがわかっている．
　まとめると，神経細胞が外（βアミロイドタンパク質の沈着）と内（神経原線維変化）から攻撃を受け，脳から脱落していき，認知力が低下してしまうのがアルツハイマー病といえる．

表　家族性アルツハイマー病と遺伝子

遺伝子名	位置	特徴
APP（βアミロイド前駆体タンパク質）遺伝子	21番染色体	APPとは，βアミロイドタンパク質のもとになるタンパク質である．APPの特定の部分が切断されて，βアミロイドタンパク質となる．APP遺伝子にわずかな変異が生じただけで，必ずアルツハイマー病になる．その意味で，これはアルツハイマー病の原因遺伝子といってよい．
アポリポタンパク質E4遺伝子（APOE4遺伝子）	19番染色体	アポリポタンパク質Eは，脳で脂質の運搬や組織の修復に関与している．このタンパク質には，アミノ酸配列に多型が見られるので，いくつかのタイプにわかれる．E4はそのうちの1つを指す．このE4タイプをつくり出す遺伝子をもつと，遅発性型の家族性アルツハイマー病にかかりやすくなるとされている．「かかりやすくなる」というだけなので，原因遺伝子とはいえない．
プレセニリンⅠ遺伝子	14番染色体	どちらも家族性アルツハイマー病の原因遺伝子である．これらの遺伝子は，細胞内輸送やカルシウムイオンの調節に関わっているとされている．
プレセニリンⅡ遺伝子	1番染色体	

解答

問1　【解答例】 13

【解説】
【2段落】を読めば解答できるようになっている．
a　肺炎で死ぬことが多い．⇒　○
　　【2段落】の最終文．肺炎＝pneumonia
b　発症後すぐから，記憶が急激に衰える．⇒　×
　　【2段落】の第1文に反する
c　迷子になりやすい．⇒　○
　　【2段落】becomes easily lost in all but the best-known surroundings.
　　（all but … ＝…を除くすべて）
d　偏執的になることがある．⇒　○
　　【2段落】Even the personality changes; the patient loses social skills and may become paranoid.
　　paranoid＝偏執的な

問 2 【解答例】2

【解説】
【3 段落】～【5 段落】までを読めば解答できる.
a 脳の X 線写真で診断できる. ⇒ ×
　【3 段落】の第 2 文：There is no blood test or X-ray study <u>with which to confirm the clinical suspicion.</u>（下線の「前置詞＋関係代名詞 + to do」という形に注意．特殊な形だが，「前置詞＋関係代名詞」の部分は無視して，to do の部分を直前の名詞，ここでは blood test や X-ray study に，かけて訳せばよい．不定詞の形容詞用法に近くなる．）
b 85 歳以上の半数がアルツハイマー病の兆候・症状をもつ. ⇒ ○
　【4 段落】の第 3 文「Some studies indicate that almost one-half of those over the age of 85 have signs and symptoms compatible with AD.」を参照.
c アルミニウムの脳への蓄積が原因である. ⇒ ×
　【5 段落】の第 1 文～第 3 文を併せて読めば，本文はアルミニウム説に否定的であることがわかる.
d 過剰の銅・亜鉛が重要な役割をはたしている可能性は否定された. ⇒ ×
　【5 段落】の後半を読むと，可能性が否定されたとはいえないことがわかる.

問 3 【解答例】13

【解説】
【6 段落】～【9 段落】に目を通さないといけない.
a 第 21 番染色体を余分にもつことで発症するダウン症候群の患者は，50 歳を超えるとそのほとんどがアルツハイマー病になる. ⇒ ○
　【7 段落】の内容と合致するとみてよいであろう.
b 第 1 番染色体にあるアミロイド前駆体タンパク質遺伝子が変異してアルツハイマー病を発症することがある. ⇒ ×
　【8 段落】を読むと，アミロイド前駆体タンパク質遺伝子は 21 番染色体上にあることがわかる.
c 40 ～ 50 歳代でアルツハイマー病を発症する人たちは遺伝子の変異が原因である可能性が高い. ⇒ ○
　【6 段落】の第 1 文を読むと，早期発症型のアルツハイマー病は遺伝しているという可能性が読み取れる.
d ボルガ - ゲルマンの遺伝的背景をもつ人々は，1 番染色体上のプレセニリン 2 に異常があることでアルツハイマー病を早期に発症することがある. ⇒ ○
　【9 段落】の「Mutations in PS2 explain the early onset of AD in a cluster of fami-

lies of Volga-German background.」を参照すればよい．

問4 【解答例】 11

【解説】
a　APOE はコレステロールを輸送するタンパク質をコードしている．⇒　○
　【10段落】の「By 1993, a team at Duke University showed that the gene in question was APOE, already well studied because it coded for a cholesterol transport protein.」を参照すればよい．
b　第19番染色体上にある．⇒　○
　【9段落】の最終文を参照．
c　APOE には，E2，E3，E4 が知られる．⇒　○
　【10段落】を参照すれば解答できる．
d　APOE の E4 タイプをもつヒトは 40～50 歳代でアルツハイマー病を発症する場合が多い．⇒　×
　【9段落】の最後の2文や，【12段落】の「Current estimates are that APOE status explains about 50% of the genetic effect on risk for late-onset disease.」を読めばわかるように，APOE は遅発性（晩期発症型）のアルツハイマー病とかかわっている．よって，「40～50 歳代」がおかしい．「40～50 歳代」だと，早期発症型アルツハイマー病の話になってしまう．

問5 【解答例】 15

【解説】
【10段落】と【11段落】が読めれば解答できる．
a　コーカシアンのうち，2～3% が APOE4 を 2 コピーもち，2 コピーもたないヒトよりもアルツハイマー病を発症しやすい．⇒　○
　次の2つの文を参考にすればよい．
1)【10段落】の最終文：Large family studies soon showed that of the three common forms of the gene (E2, E3, and E4, which are found on 7%, 78%, and 15% of chromosomes among Caucasians), E4 was associated with risk for AD.
2)【11段落】の第1文：The most important discovery was that the 2-3% (a number arrived at by multiplying 15% by 15% because the chance of inheriting a copy from one parent is independent of the chance of inheriting a copy from another parent) of persons born with two copies of APOE4 were far more likely to have AD than were age-matched controls who did not have two copies.
　　下線部には注意．「be likely to do … ＝…する可能性がある」という表現は非常に

重要である．この表現は，比較級と一緒によく使われるという点も注意しておきたい．than 以下は，SV という語順ではなく，VS という語順になっている．「than V S」という形はしばしば出てくるので捉え違いをしてはいけない．S が長くなる場合に，この倒置形が登場することが多い．

b APOE2 はアルツハイマー病を予防している．⇒ ○
【11 段落】の「Other studies showed that E2 seemed to protect against AD.」を参照すればよい．

c APOE2 を 2 コピーもつヒトはアルツハイマー病になりにくいか，もたない人より発症が遅いと考えられている．⇒ ○
【11 段落】の最終文を参照すればよい．

d APOE4 遺伝子は，コーカシアンの第 19 番染色体の 15％に見つかる．⇒ ○
【10 段落】の最終文を参照すればよい．

問 6 【解答例】8

【解説】

a APOE だけではアルツハイマー病のリスクを予見することはできない．⇒ ×
【12 段落】の第 1 文の捉え方が問題となる．第 1 文の前半では，APOE がもっとも重大な危険因子だと述べられているので，「APOE だけでリスクを予見することができない」と言い切るのは，無理であろう．APOE だけでもある程度のリスクを予見することはできるが，「スクリーニング検査に使えるほど十分な予見可能性はない」（【12 段落】の第 1 文の後半）といっているだけと考えればよいと思う．よって，ここでは，本文の内容と合致しないと考えた．

b APOE4 をもつヒトでもアルツハイマー病を発症しない場合がある．⇒ ○
【12 段落】の第 2 文に合致する．

c APOE4 をもたないヒトでもアルツハイマー病を発症する場合がある．⇒ ○
【12 段落】の第 2 文に合致する．

d 40 ～ 50 歳代でアルツハイマー病を発症する場合の 50％は，APOE4 で説明できる．⇒ ×
【12 段落】の「Current estimates are that APOE status explains about 50% of the genetic effect on risk for late-onset disease.」に反する．本文では，40 ～ 50 歳代での発症は「late-onset disease」に相当しない．

問 7 【解答例】12

【解説】

a アルツハイマー病の患者を家系内にもつヒトは APOE4 の遺伝子を調べるべきである．

⇒ ○

【14 段落】の第 2 文では，遺伝子を調べることに否定的なことが述べられている．しかし，第 3 文の冒頭を見ると，「However」という逆接の言葉があるので，第 3 文以降は，遺伝子を調べることに肯定的な意見が表明されていることになる．そして，第 6 文で，親が APOE4 をもっている場合には，検査を受けるとよい場合があると述べられている．

b　アルツハイマー病の治療法が確立していないのに APOE4 などの遺伝子診断を行うことには，倫理的な問題がある．⇒ ○

【15 段落】の最後から 2 つ目の文である「Since the disease is incurable, if such a test is developed, it will be engulfed in ethical debate.」を参考にして，本文に合致していると考えた．

engulf ＝〜を巻き込む，〜を飲み込む．

c　最初の質問，「*My mom, who is in a nursing home, developed Alzheimer's disease at age 74. How high is my risk*?」には，家族にアルツハイマー病の人がいない場合よりは確実に高いと答える．⇒ ×

【15 段落】の第 1 文の「one can say little more than that it probably suggests a somewhat greater risk to the children than if there was no family history.」をどう解釈するかが問題となる．とくに，「it probably suggests」の部分が問題である．probably は，「おそらく」「十中八九」という意味である．よって，「確実に」という言葉が使われている選択肢 c は本文と合致しないと考える．probably の代わりに，certainly が使われていれば，本文と合致しているといえるであろう．

d　炎症には中心的な役割をはたす IL-1 をコードする遺伝子の変異は新たな遺伝的要因である可能性がある．⇒ ○

【12 段落】の最終文に合致する．

p.62【問題 19】 鹿児島大学　平成15年

問題の特徴

下線部和訳はなく，内容説明問題だけである．問1と問2は下線部がないので，最初から文を読んで解答に必要な箇所を見つける必要がある．問3と問4は下線部つきである．こちらは，確率的にいって下線部のすぐ近くに解答に必要な箇所がある場合が多い．本問もそうである．

本文のテーマ

感染症の脅威を述べている文章である．抗生物質やワクチンのおかげで感染症の脅威は緩和されたとはいえ，結局，人類は周期的になんらかの感染症に襲われて被害を受けることを避けられないという内容．題材としては，インフルエンザのパンデミックや新興感染症の1つであるSARSが出てくる．

1　インフルエンザウイルスとパンデミック（世界的大流行）

(1)　インフルエンザウイルス

A型とB型とC型があるが，ヒトに感染して猛威をふるうのはA型である．A型インフルエンザウイルスの表面には，ヘマグルチニン（H1～H16の16種類）とノイラミニダーゼ（N1～N9の9種類）という2つの糖タンパク質が存在している．よって，理論的には144種類のA型インフルエンザウイルスが存在することになる．2009年に世界的流行したのはH1N1型であった．

(2)　遺伝子再集合（reassortment）

インフルエンザウイルスがパンデミックを引き起こすしくみとして有名な現象が，遺伝子再集合である．遺伝子再集合とは，2つの類似のウイルスが同じ細胞に感染した際に，お互いの遺伝物質が混ざり合って新しいウイルスが誕生する現象である．下記の図を参考にしてほしい．アルファベットはインフルエンザウイルスがもつ遺伝子を表している．

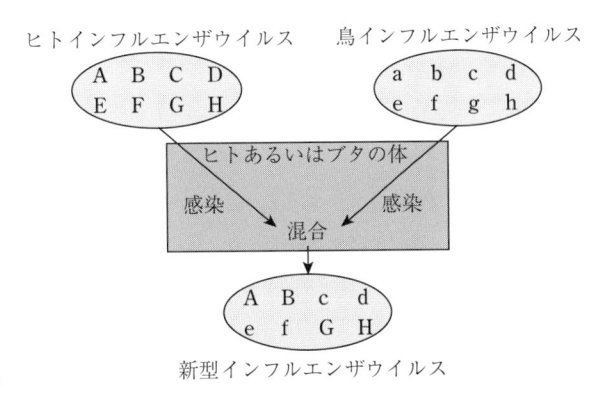

2　新興感染症

(1)　定義

新興感染症とは，「かつて知られていなかった，新しく認識された感染症で，局地的に，あるいは，国際的に，公衆衛生上問題となる感染症」のことである．1970年代以降だけ

でも 30 種類以上が確認されている．

(2) 典型例
ウイルス感染症：SARS，エイズ，エボラ出血熱，鳥インフルエンザ（H5N1）
細菌感染症：レジオネラ症，出血性大腸炎（病原性大腸菌 O157）
その他：BSE（ウシ海綿状脳症）

(3) 新興感染症が流行する背景
・森林開発 ⇒ 野生動物との接触 ⇒ 動物に由来する新たな病原微生物が人に広まる（SARS を引き起こすコロナウイルスも，コウモリに由来することがわかっている）．
・世界的な人の動きが活発化した（交通の発達）．
・人口の都市集中化

〔参考〕再興感染症
　既知の感染症で，すでに公衆衛生上問題とならない程度にまで患者数が減少していた感染症のうち，ふたたび流行しはじめ，患者数が増加したもの．自然破壊，地球温暖化，予防接種の不徹底，耐性菌の出現などが原因である．
典型例：結核，ジフテリア，マラリア，狂犬病など

解答
問1【解答例】 運がかなり良かったことと，懸命な科学的努力がなされたこと，ウイルスを封じ込める迅速な措置が取られたことが理由として挙げられる．

【解説】
　設問の「1997年」「香港」という言葉を意識して本文を読んでいけば，【3段落】が解答に関連していそうなことがわかるであろう．具体的にいうと，【3段落】の第2文を訳せれば解答できる．
【3段落】の第2文：Much luck, hard scientific labor ① and prompt containment measures ② prevented that outbreak from turning into a global catastrophe.
⇒下線①：and を使って単語や語句を列挙する際には，最後のものの前にだけ and をおけばよい．ここも3つ列挙されているが，最後にきている，prompt containment measures の前にしか and はない．この and の用法は非常にたくさん出てくるので注意しておきたい．
⇒下線②：「prevent O from doing…＝ O が…するのを妨げる」という必須表現が出てきている．学士試験といえども，こうした基本表現を知っていれば確実に得点できる．

問2【解答例】 第一次世界大戦中に，軍隊の陣営や輸送機関や塹壕の中でたくさんの人が

密集していたことが，理由として挙げられる．

【解説】
「1918年のスペイン型インフルエンザが広範囲に流行」という設問の言葉に対応しているのは，【5段落】の第1文の冒頭であろう．この第1文をさらに読むと，「異常なまでにスペイン型インフルエンザが広がったのは，第一次世界大戦と関連がある」と書かれている．具体的な関連性は，which以降を読むとはっきりとわかってくる．「crowed together（一緒になって密集していた）」という単語がポイントになる．
〔補足〕seeの少し変わった使い方
The 18th century saw the American Revolution.（18世紀には米国独立戦争が起こった）
⇒主語に時代や出来事がくる場合がある．

問3【解答例】 6年前に発生した鳥インフルエンザの原因となったウイルスの変異型が，中国南部で出現していること．また，まったく別の系統のインフルエンザウイルスが生じて，世界的大流行が起こる可能性もあるということも根拠として挙げられる．実際に，江蘇省や珠江デルタでは，他の種に存在しているそれぞれのインフルエンザウイルスに接触したということを示唆するような抗体ができている農民が発見された．だから，それらのウイルスの1つが人間に適合し，広がるのは時間の問題といえる．

【解説】
まずは下線部の内容をしっかりつかむこと．下線部の内容を簡単にまとめると，「またパンデミックが起こることは確実である．それが，中国の南部で始まる可能性が高い」ということになる．このように考える根拠は，下線部の次の文に書かれている．この文のor以降で述べられていること（まったく別の系統のインフルエンザウイルスが発生する）の理由となる事実が【7段落】に述べられていると考え，【7段落】も解答に含めている．【7段落】では，いろいろな種のインフルエンザウイルスに接触したと見られる農民が出てくる．このように，1つの個体内に数種類のインフルエンザウイルスが混在する状態になると，再集合という現象が起こり，まったく新しいインフルエンザウイルスが生じる可能性が高まる．

問4【解答例】 新たな感染症の脅威により，以前と同じように自然のなすがままになっている人類の状態を示している．人類はこれまでも，インフルエンザという感染症の大流行に翻弄され，大きな被害を受けてきた．さらに今また，空気感染を起こせば，1918年のインフルエンザと同じくらいの被害を出すといわれているSARSの脅威にさらされている．SARSが別の種に由来する病気ということがわかれば，薬やワクチンが作れるかもしれない．だが，それらを作れたとしても，完成する頃までに致命的な損害が出てしまっているだろう．こう考えると，人類は新しい感染症に，以前と同じように翻弄されており，

自然のなすがままといえる．(288字)

【解説】
　下線部②を含む英文（【8段落】の最終文）は，「以前と同じように，自分たちが自然のなすがままになっていることに気づく」という意味である．【8段落】を読むと，インフルエンザの脅威にさらされてきた人類が，今また，SARSという新たな感染症の脅威にさらされてなすすべがないという状況が描かれている．下線部②は，この状況を「自然のなすがままになっている」と表現している．

〔補足〕【8段落】の第2文，第3文の捉え方
第2文：Perhaps if we (1)<u>knew</u> that SARS had come from another species, we (2)<u>could identify</u> how it had changed and we could design drugs or vaccines to tackle it.
第3文：By the time we (3)<u>had produced</u> them, however, the disease (4)<u>would already have done</u> its deadly damage.
和訳：おそらく，もし，SARSが別の種から生じたものだったということがわかれば，私たちはそれがどのように変異したのかを特定し，それに対処するための薬やワクチンを設計できるだろう．しかし，私たちがそれらを作れたとしても，その頃までに，その病気はすでに致死的な被害をもたらしてしまっていたであろう．

　この箇所の概要をしっかりつかむことが重要．ようするに「人類がSARSという新しい感染症に翻弄されている」ということを述べている．
　第2文の下線(1)(2)を見ると，仮定法過去の形になっていることがわかる．よって，ここでは「現時点では，SARSが別の種から生じたのかはわかっておらず，薬やワクチンを作ることは実際にはできない」ということが述べられていることになる．
　第3文の下線(3)(4)を見ると，仮定法過去完了（過去の事実に反する仮定）の形に似ているという印象を受ける．上記の和訳もこの視点で作成したものである．ようするに「過去において実際には薬やワクチンは作られなかったが，もし作られていたとしても，その頃までには，致命的な被害が出てしまっていたであろう」という捉え方である．
　しかし，第3文は未来のことを仮定していると考えてもよいように見える．つまり，直前の第2文の内容と合わせて考えてみると，「現段階では，私たちは薬やワクチンは作れない．そして，今後もし仮にそれらを作れたとしても，その頃までには，致命的な被害が出てしまっているだろう」と解釈してみたくもなる．ただし，下線(3)は未来のことを述べる形ではないので（下線(4)は未来のことを表せる可能性もある），文法的な説明が難しくなる．
　結局，第3文はかなり難しい文だが，あまり深く考えずに，「薬やワクチンが作れたとしても，大きな被害が出てしまう」という基本的な内容が理解できればよいだろう．
〔語句〕at the mercy of ～ ＝ ～のなすがまま（controlled by ～）

重要単語リスト

§1 テーマ別重要単語リスト

ここでは，各テーマに関連した専門的な単語を列挙していく．

1 細胞

	単語	意味
1	with the naked eye	肉眼で
2	eukaryotic cell	真核細胞
3	prokaryotic cell	原核細胞
4	somatic cell	体細胞
5	germ (reproductive) cell	生殖細胞
6	organelle	細胞小器官
7	nucleus	核
8	nuclear envelope	核膜（＝nuclear membrane）
9	chromosome	染色体
10	cytoplasm	細胞質
11	plasma membrane	細胞膜
12	mitochondria	ミトコンドリア
13	be embedded in ～	～に埋め込まれている
14	permeable	透過性のある
15	diffusion	拡散
16	osmosis	浸透
17	concentration gradient	濃度勾配
18	passive transport	受動輸送
19	active transport	能動輸送
20	gene	遺伝子
21	replication	複製（＝duplication）
22	transcription	転写
23	cell division	細胞分裂
24	meiosis	減数分裂
25	progeny cell	娘細胞
26	stem cell	幹細胞
27	regenerative medicine	再生医療
28	tissue engineering	組織工学
29	birth defect	先天性異常
30	differentiate	分化する

2 組織・器官

	単語	意味
1	flesh	肉（骨・皮に対する）
2	tissue	組織
3	organ	器官，臓器
4	sensory receptor	感覚器
5	olfactory	嗅覚の
6	optic	目の，視覚の，光学の
7	retina	網膜
8	cornea	角膜
9	auditory	耳の，聴覚の
10	epithelial tissue	上皮組織
11	connective tissue	結合組織
12	muscular tissue	筋肉組織
13	nervous tissue	神経組織
14	adipose tissue	脂肪組織
15	brain	脳
16	cerebrum	大脳
17	cerebral cortex	大脳皮質
18	hippocampus	海馬
19	hypothalamus	視床下部
20	neuron	神経細胞，ニューロン
21	spinal cord	脊髄
22	spine	脊椎
23	nerve	神経
24	ligament	靭帯
25	tendon	腱
26	cartilage	軟骨
27	thigh	太もも
28	skeletal muscle	骨格筋
29	cardiac muscle	心筋
30	contract	収縮する，病気にかかる
31	elastic	伸縮性のある
32	digestive system	消化系
33	salivary glands	唾液腺
34	liver	肝臓
35	hepatic	肝臓の
36	hepatitis	肝炎
37	pancreas	膵臓
38	intestine	腸
39	stomach	胃
40	gastric	胃の
41	digestion	消化
42	ingest	摂取する
43	intake	摂食

44	saliva	唾液
45	central nervous system	中枢神経系
46	peripheral nervous system	末梢神経系
47	somatic nervous system	体性神経系
48	autonomic nervous system	自律神経系
49	circulatory system	循環系
50	lung	肺
51	inhale	吸い込む，吸入
52	exhale	吐き出す
53	lodge	詰まる
54	cardiac	心臓の
55	atrium	心房
56	ventricle	心室
57	artery	動脈
58	vein	静脈
59	blood vessel	血管
60	capillary	毛細血管
61	cardiovascular	心臓血管の
62	coronary arteries	冠動脈
63	circulate	循環する
64	plasma	血漿
65	erythrocyte	赤血球
66	leukocyte	白血球
67	platelet	血小板
68	bone marrow	骨髄
69	umbilical cord	臍の緒
70	cord blood	臍帯血
71	sickle-cell anemia	鎌状赤血球貧血症
72	endocrine system	内分泌系
73	exocrine system	外分泌系
74	thyroid	甲状腺
75	adrenal gland	副腎
76	secrete	分泌する
77	dwarf	小人
78	kidney	腎臓
79	urine	尿
80	excretion	排出，排泄
81	reproductive system	生殖系
82	prostate gland	前立腺
83	ovaries（ovary の複数形）	卵巣
84	uterus	子宮（＝womb）
85	placenta	胎盤
86	fertilization	受精
87	fertilized egg	受精卵
88	gamete	配偶子

89	sperm	精子
90	embryo	胚
91	embryonic	胚の
92	fetus	胎児
93	pelvis	骨盤
94	chest	胸
95	thoracic	胸部の
96	abdomen	腹部
97	abdominal	腹部の
98	dorsal	背部の，背面の
99	posterior	後の，後部の
100	anterior	前の，前部の

3　医学分野・専門科

	単語	意味
1	anatomy	解剖（学），解剖学的構造
2	ecology	生態学
3	epidemiology	疫学，伝染病学
4	geriatrics	老人病学，老年医学
5	geriatric care	老人介護
6	gerontology	老年学
7	genetics	遺伝学
8	histology	組織学
9	senescence	老化
10	immunology	免疫学
11	pathology	病理学，病理
12	pharmacology	薬理学
13	physiology	生理学，生理（機能）
14	internal medicine	内科
15	physician	内科医
16	obstetrics and gynecology	産科（学）及び婦人科（学）
17	obstetrician	産科医
18	gynecologist	婦人科医
19	maternity ward	産科病棟
20	pediatrics	小児科（学）
21	pediatrician	小児科医
22	dermatology	皮膚科（学）
23	psychiatry	精神科（学）
24	psychiatrist	精神科医
25	surgery	外科（学）
26	surgeon	外科医
27	orthopedics	整形外科（学）
28	plastic surgery	形成外科（学），美容外科（学）
29	radiology	放射線科（学）
30	radiologist	放射線科医

31	veterinary medicine	獣医学
32	veterinarian	獣医
33	dentist	歯科医
34	midwife	助産師
35	pharmacist	薬剤師
36	dietitian（or dietician）	栄養士
37	health professional	医療従事者

4　公衆衛生

	単語	意味
1	population	集団，個体群，人口
2	aging society	高齢化社会
3	average life expectancy	平均余命
4	average life span	平均寿命
5	blood donation	献血
6	carcinogen	発癌物質
7	childcare leave	育児休暇
8	contamination	汚染
9	disabled	身体障害のある
10	food sanitation	食品衛生
11	health insurance	健康保険
12	hygiene	衛生
13	fitness	健康
14	disability	障害
15	nutrition	栄養（＝nourishment）
16	intake	摂取
17	metabolism	代謝
18	malpractice	医療過誤
19	maternity leave	産休
20	medical expenses	医療費
21	suicide	自殺
22	fertility rate	出生率
23	mortality	死亡率
24	morbidity	疾病率
25	nursing home	老人ホーム，介護施設
26	nursery	託児所，子供部屋
27	organ donor	臓器提供者
28	organ recipient	臓器移植者（臓器移植を受ける人）
29	pollution	汚染
30	quarantine	検疫所，隔離する，検疫する
31	sewage disposal	下水処理
32	vaccination	予防接種
33	immunization	予防接種
34	inoculation	予防接種
35	neonate	新生児

36	infancy	幼児期
37	puberty	思春期
38	juvenile	若年性の，若い，少年少女の
39	adolescence	青年期
40	senescence	老年期，老化，老齢
41	child-bearing age	出産適齢期
42	additive	食品添加物
43	chemical preservative	合成保存料
44	poll	世論調査
45	advocacy group	擁護団体，支援団体
46	early detection	早期発見
47	laboratory	実験室，研究室
48	fund	資金を提供する
49	subsidy	補助金
50	grant	助成金
51	incidence	発生率
52	prevalence	有病率
53	hygiene hypothesis	衛生仮説

5　検査・医療機材

	単語	意味
1	autopsy	検死
2	biopsy	生体組織検査
3	mammogram	乳房X線写真
4	negative	陰性の　　cf. false-negative＝偽陰性の
5	positive	陽性の　　cf. false-positive＝偽陽性の
6	sensitivity	感度（患者が病気にかかっている場合に検査結果が陽性になる確率）
7	specificity	特異度（患者が病気にかかっていない場合に検査結果が陰性になる確率）
8	neutral fat	中性脂肪
9	palpation	触診
10	PET（positron emission tomography）	陽電子放出（型）断層撮影（法）
11	physical examination	健康診断
12	physical checkup	健康診断
13	specimen	標本
14	stool examination	便検査
15	ambulance	救急車
16	dialysis	透析
17	bandage	包帯
18	delivery table	分娩台
19	diaper	おむつ
20	endoscope	内視鏡
21	false teeth	入れ歯
22	hearing aid	補聴器
23	life-support system	生命維持装置

24	microscope	顕微鏡
25	respirator	人工呼吸器
26	ventilator	人工呼吸器
27	stethoscope	聴診器
28	syringe	注射器
29	thermometer	温度計
30	tweezers	ピンセット
31	wheelchair	車椅子
32	acute	急性の
33	chronic	慢性の
34	alert	感覚や意識がよく働いている，覚醒している
35	alleviate	緩和する
36	benign	良性の
37	malignant	悪性の
38	contagious	伝染性の
39	congenital	先天性の
40	critical condition	危篤状態
41	findings	所見，発見，研究結果
42	incubation period	潜伏期間（＝latent period）
43	infectious	感染性の
44	manifestation	病気の徴候
45	outcome	転帰（病気の治療後の結果）
46	previous disease	既往症
47	prognosis	予後
48	recurrence	再発
49	remission	寛解
50	metastasis	転移
51	stable condition	小康状態
52	symptom	症状
53	isolate	単離する
54	defibrillator	除細動器

6　治験（臨床試験）

	単語	意味
1	clinical trial	治験，臨床試験
2	subject	被験者
3	Phase I Trial	第1相試験
4	Phase II Trial	第2相試験
5	Phase III Trial	第3相試験
6	control group	対照群
7	double-blind	二重盲検法，二重盲検の
8	randomized	ランダム化された，無作為に抽出された
9	end point	（臨床試験における）評価項目
10	placebo effect	プラセボ効果

7　治療・薬

	単語	意味
1	acupuncture	鍼治療
2	alternative medicine	代替療法
3	anesthesia	麻酔，麻酔薬
4	blood transfusion	輸血
5	chemotherapy	化学療法
6	cosmetic surgery	美容外科
7	CPR（cardiopulmonary resuscitation）	心肺蘇生
8	disinfection	消毒
9	sterilization	消毒
10	eradication	根絶
11	first aid	応急手当て
12	hypodermic injection	皮下注射
13	intravenous injection	静脈注射
14	IV（＝intravenous）	点滴
15	medical procedure	医療処置
16	criterion（複数形は，criteria）	基準
17	physical therapy	理学療法
18	radiotherapy	放射線医療
19	stitch	縫合する
20	incision	切開
21	surgery	外科手術
22	tablet	錠剤
23	agent	薬剤，物質
24	anesthetic	麻酔薬
25	antibiotic	抗生物質
26	antidepressant	抗うつ剤
27	contraceptive	避妊薬
28	birth-control pill	経口避妊薬
29	fertility drug	排卵誘発剤
30	immunosuppressive drug	免疫抑制剤
31	inhibitor	阻害剤
32	laxative	下剤
33	oral medicine	経口薬
34	over-the-counter medicine	市販薬
35	prescription drug	処方薬
36	pharmaceutical	薬剤，薬剤の，薬剤師の
37	medication	薬物治療
38	sedative	鎮静剤
39	sleeping pill	睡眠薬
40	agonist	作動薬（受容体に結合し，生体内物質と同様の細胞内情報伝達系を作動させる薬物）
41	antagonist	拮抗薬（何かの作用を邪魔する薬）
42	dose	投与量，服用量
43	dosage	服用量

44	adherence	服薬遵守（＝compliance）
45	drug abuse	薬物濫用
46	drug addiction	薬物中毒
47	drug dependence	薬物依存
48	drug resistance	薬剤耐性
49	expiration date	使用期限，消費期限
50	lethal dose	致死量
51	side effect	副作用
52	muscular relaxant	筋弛緩剤
53	toxic	毒性の　　cf. toxicity＝毒性
54	venom	毒

8　病気

	単語	意味
1	ailment	病気
2	malady	病気
3	infirmity	病気
4	asthma	喘息
5	bronchitis	気管支炎
6	common cold	風邪
7	malignant neoplasm	悪性新生物
8	lung cancer	肺がん
9	pneumonia	肺炎
10	COPD（chronic obstructive pulmonary disease）	慢性閉塞性肺疾患
11	tuberculosis	結核
12	hardening of the arteries	動脈硬化
13	heart attack	心臓発作
14	heart failure	心不全
15	myocardial infarction	心筋梗塞
16	cardiovascular disease	心臓血管疾患
17	coronary heart disease	冠動脈心疾患
18	anemia	貧血
19	hemophilia	血友病
20	leukemia	白血病
21	brain hemorrhage	脳出血
22	stroke	脳卒中
23	bovine spongiform encephalopathy	牛海綿状脳症（BSE）
24	epilepsy	てんかん
25	muscular dystrophy	筋ジストロフィー
26	appendicitis	虫垂炎
27	gastric ulcer	胃潰瘍
28	hepatitis	肝炎
29	inflammation of the mouth	口内炎
30	STD（sexually transmitted disease）	性感染症
31	syphilis	梅毒

32	urinary tract infection	尿路感染症
33	breast cancer	乳がん
34	menopause	閉経，更年期
35	menopausal disorder	更年期障害
36	uterine cancer	子宮がん
37	cataract	白内障
38	glaucoma	緑内障
39	color blindness	色盲，色覚異常
40	nearsightedness	近視
41	night blindness	夜盲症
42	deaf	耳が聞こえない
43	dumb	口がきけない（＝mute）
44	impaired hearing	難聴
45	arthritis	関節炎
46	fracture	骨折
47	osteoporosis	骨粗鬆症
48	sprain	捻挫
49	abrasion	擦り傷
50	bruise	打撲
51	burn	火傷
52	insect bite	虫さされ
53	rupture	破裂，ヘルニア
54	scar	傷跡
55	fatal wound	致命傷
56	athlete's foot	水虫
57	wart	いぼ
58	ADHD（attention-deficit hyperactivity disorder）	注意欠陥多動性障害
59	chicken pox	水痘
60	measles	はしか
61	mumps	おたふく風邪
62	autism	自閉症
63	dementia	認知症
64	mental disorder	精神障害
65	depression	うつ病
66	burnout	燃え尽き症候群
67	eating disorder	摂食障害
68	gender identity disorder	性同一性障害
69	obsession	強迫観念
70	psychosomatic disorder	心身症
71	insomnia	不眠症
72	schizophrenia	統合失調症
73	anorexia	拒食症
74	AIDS（acquired immune deficiency syndrome）	後天性免疫不全症候群
75	aftereffect	後遺症
76	complication	合併症

77	diabetes	糖尿病
78	food poisoning	食中毒
79	hay fever	花粉症（＝pollinosis）
80	genetic disease	遺伝病
81	leprosy	ハンセン病
82	lifestyle-related disease	生活習慣病
83	tetanus	破傷風
84	malnutrition	栄養失調
85	occupational disease	職業病
86	plague	疫病
87	PTSD（posttraumatic stress disorder）	心的外傷後ストレス障害
88	rabies	狂犬病
89	radiation exposure	放射線被ばく
90	scurvy	壊血病
91	rickets	くる病
92	vitamin deficiency disease	ビタミン欠乏症
93	sepsis	敗血症
94	smallpox	天然痘
95	sunstroke	日射病
96	suicide	自殺
97	cadaver	死体
98	brain death	脳死
99	cardiac death	心臓死
100	euthanasia	安楽死
101	death with dignity	尊厳死
102	immediate death	即死
103	starvation	餓死，飢え
104	suffocation	窒息

9　症状

	単語	意味
1	symptom	症状
2	diagnosis	診断
3	misdiagnosis	誤診
4	fitness	健康
5	bedfast	寝たきりの
6	bedridden	寝たきりの
7	coma	昏睡
8	fainting	気絶すること
9	headache	頭痛
10	sore	痛い（形容詞）　例：a sore throat
11	hurt	痛い（動詞），～を傷つける（を怪我する）
12	migraine	偏頭痛
13	vertigo	めまい
14	allergic reaction	アレルギー反応

15	cough	咳
16	sputum, phlegm	痰
17	nosebleed	鼻血
18	snoring	いびき
19	itching	かゆみ
20	wheezing	ぜいぜい息をすること
21	sneezing	くしゃみ
22	have a runny nose	鼻水が出る
23	blood clot	血栓
24	cardiac arrest	心停止
25	hypertension	高血圧
26	hypotension	低血圧
27	appetite loss	食欲不振
28	bloody stool	血便
29	constipation	便秘
30	diarrhea	下痢
31	feces	便
32	heartburn	胸焼け
33	indigestion	消化不良
34	nausea	吐き気
35	stomachache	腹痛
36	vomiting	嘔吐
37	bloody urine	血尿
38	frequent urination	頻尿
39	lump	（乳房の）しこり
40	muscle spasm	筋肉の痙攣
41	deformity	奇形
42	numbness	しびれ
43	paralysis	麻痺
44	trembling	震え
45	shivering	震え
46	eczema	湿疹
47	mole	ほくろ
48	tan	日焼け
49	rash	発疹
50	erupt	噴火する，発疹が出る
51	baldness	はげ
52	chill	寒気
53	convulsion	痙攣
54	dizziness	めまい
55	drowsiness	眠気
56	dullness	だるさ
57	hangover	二日酔い
58	habitual	常習的な
59	beverage	飲料

60	dysfunction	機能不全
61	fever	熱
62	fatigue	疲労
63	infertility	不妊症
64	inflammation	炎症
65	irritation	炎症
66	necrosis	壊死
67	rejection	拒絶反応
68	swelling	腫れ
69	swollen	腫れている
70	tumor	腫瘍
71	withdrawal symptoms	禁断症状
72	chronic	慢性の
73	acute	急性の
74	local	局所的な
75	systemic	全身の
76	congenital	先天性の
77	acquired	後天性の
78	terminal	末期の

10 癌

	単語	意味
1	benign tumor	良性腫瘍
2	malignant tumor	悪性腫瘍
3	biological therapy	生物（学的）療法：treatment to stimulate or restore the ability of the immune system to fight infection and disease. also called immunotherapy.
4	chemotherapy	化学療法：treatment with anticancer drugs.
5	hormone therapy	ホルモン療法：treatment of cancer by changing hormone levels.
6	biopsy	生体組織検査：removal of a sample of tissue, which is then examined under a microscope to check for cancer cells
7	bone marrow transplantation	骨髄移植
8	cancer	癌
9	carcinogen	発癌物質：a substance or agent that is known to cause cancer.
10	cervical	（子宮）頸部の　　cf. cervical cancer＝子宮頸癌
11	edema	浮腫，水腫
12	epithelial	上皮の
13	gene therapy	遺伝子治療
14	hysterectomy	子宮摘出術
15	incise	切開する（incision＝切開）
16	invasive cancer	浸潤癌：cancers that are capable of growing beyond their site of origin and invading surrounding tissue.
17	laparoscopy	腹腔鏡手術
18	leukemia	白血病
19	local treatment of cancer	癌の局所療法：treatment of the tumor only.
20	mammogram	マンモグラム（乳房X線写真）

21	mastectomy	乳房切除術：surgery to remove the breast.
22	metastasis	転移
23	oncology	腫瘍学
24	palliative therapy	緩和治療
25	radical treatment	根治治療（definitive treatment でもよい）
26	symptomatic treatment	対症療法

11 肥満

	単語	意味
1	adipose tissue	脂肪組織
2	bariatrics	肥満学（肥満の治療・予防を研究する分野）
3	bariatric surgery	肥満（症治療）手術
4	body mass index（BMI）	体格指数：「体重（kg）÷身長（m）の2乗」→アメリカでは BMI が 30 以上だと obesity（肥満）ということになる.
5	obese	肥満の
6	obesity	肥満（BMI が 30 以上）→日本では BMI が 25 以上だと肥満となる.
7	overweight	太りすぎの（正常な体重ではないが，肥満でもない状態）→アメリカでは BMI が 25～30 未満の場合を指す.
8	breastfeeding	母乳育児
9	bulimia	過食症 ⇔ anorexia（拒食症）
10	carbohydrate	炭水化物
11	fat	脂肪
12	gastric	胃の
13	gestational diabetes	妊娠性糖尿病
14	High Density Lipoprotein（HDL）	高比重リポタンパク（質）
15	Low Density Lipoprotein（LDL）	低比重リポタンパク（質）
16	leptin	レプチン：中枢神経を介して食欲を抑制するタンパク質
17	metabolism	代謝
18	saturated fat	飽和脂肪
19	unsaturated fat	不飽和脂肪
20	type 1 diabetes	1 型糖尿病
21	type 2 diabetes	2 型糖尿病
22	insulin resistance	インスリン抵抗性
23	waist circumference	腰周りの長さ

12 遺伝・ゲノム

	単語	意味
1	allele	対立遺伝子
2	locus	遺伝子座
3	nucleic acid	核酸
4	complementary base pair	相補的塩基対
5	base sequence	塩基配列
6	chromosome	染色体
7	autosome	常染色体
8	comparative genomics	比較ゲノム学
9	complex trait	複雑な形質

10	confidentiality	守秘義務, 秘密性
11	congenital	先天的な
12	diploid	2倍体（の）, 複相（の）
13	haploid	単相の, 半数体
14	disease-associated gene	疾患関連遺伝子
15	carrier	保因者
16	electrophoresis	電気泳動
17	enzyme	酵素
18	eugenics	優生学
19	eukaryote	真核生物（または真核細胞）
20	prokaryote	原核生物（または原核細胞）
21	forensics	科学捜査
22	identical twin	一卵性双生児
23	gene expression	遺伝子発現
24	genetic discrimination	遺伝子差別
25	genetic disorder	遺伝子疾患
26	genetic engineering	遺伝子工学
27	genetic polymorphism	遺伝的多型
28	genetic variant	遺伝的変異
29	genetic testing	遺伝子検査［診断・診断・分析］
30	personalized medicine	オーダーメイド医療
31	genotype	遺伝子型
32	phenotype	表現型
33	germ line gene therapy	生殖細胞系の遺伝子治療
34	somatic cell gene therapy	体細胞系の遺伝子治療
35	high-throughput sequencing	高性能配列解読装置
36	homologous chromosome	相同染色体
37	hybridization	交配
38	immunotherapy	免疫療法
39	Mendelian inheritance	メンデル遺伝
40	dominant	優性の
41	recessive	劣性の
42	meiosis	減数分裂
43	mitosis	（体細胞の核の）有糸分裂
44	model organism	モデル動物（実験動物）
45	monogenic disorder	単一遺伝子疾患
46	polygenic disorder	多遺伝子遺伝病
47	nature and nurture	生まれと育ち
48	oncogene	発癌遺伝子
49	pharmacogenomics	薬理ゲノム学（投与薬剤に対する反応性を決定する遺伝子の同定）
50	population genetics	集団遺伝学
51	recombinant DNA technology	組み換えDNA技術
52	transgenic	遺伝子組換えの
53	restriction enzyme	制限酵素
54	reverse transcriptase	逆転写酵素

55	scaffold	足場
56	segregation	分離
57	sequence	DNAを塩基配列を突き止める
58	sporadic	散発的な，孤発性の
59	transcription factor	転写因子
60	translation	翻訳

13　クローン

	単語	意味
1	clone	クローン，クローンを作る
2	somatic cell	体細胞
3	reproductive cloning	生殖型クローン
4	therapeutic cloning	治療型クローン
5	embryo	胚
6	implant	植え付ける
7	unfertilized egg	未受精卵
8	asexual reproduction	無性生殖
9	livestock	家畜
10	enucleate	除核する

14　妊娠・出産・生殖医療

	単語	意味
1	assisted reproduction technologies	生殖補助医療
2	reproductive medicine	生殖医療
3	fertility treatment（またはinfertility treatment）	不妊治療
4	reproductive right	女性の生殖に関する権利
5	IVF（in vitro fertilization）	体外受精
6	AID（artificial insemination by donor）	非配偶者間人工授精
7	prenatal diagnosis	出生前診断
8	pre-implantation genetic diagnosis	着床前遺伝子診断
9	conception , gestation, pregnancy	妊娠
10	term	出産予定日
11	trimester	妊娠期間（妊娠9カ月を3分割し，第一期（first trimester），第二期(second trimester)，第三期(third or last trimester) と呼ぶ）
12	labor	陣痛
13	Caesarean section（C-section）	帝王切開
14	delivery room	分娩室
15	multiple birth	多胎妊娠，多子出産
16	triplet	三つ子
17	procreate	子供を産む
18	adoption	養子（縁組）
19	contraception	避妊
20	abortion	中絶
21	infanticide	乳児殺し
22	pro-choice	中絶に賛成の

23	pro-life	中絶に反対の
24	viability	生存可能性，実行可能性
25	miscarriage	流産
26	teratogen	催奇形物質
27	deformed	奇形の
28	infertility	不妊
29	infertile, sterile	不妊の
30	sexually transmitted diseases	性感染症
31	fertilization	受精
32	fertilized egg	受精卵
33	implantation	着床
34	womb, uterus	子宮
35	placenta	胎盤
36	pelvic	骨盤の
37	sperm	精子
38	ovum（複数形は ova）	卵（子）
39	germ cell（または reproductive cell）	生殖細胞
40	gamete	配偶子
41	embryo	胚
42	embryology	発生学
43	spare embryo	余剰胚
44	stillbirth	死産
45	premature birth	早産
46	premature baby	未熟児
47	fetus	胎児
48	neonatal	新生児の
49	perinatal care	周産期医療
50	breast-feed	母乳で育てる
51	ovulation	排卵
52	ovulation inducing drug（または fertility drug）	排卵誘発剤
53	eugenics	優生学
54	cerebral palsy	脳性麻痺
55	anonymous	匿名の
56	fine	罰金，罰金を科す
57	fallacy	誤った考え
58	surrogate mother	代理母
59	surrogacy contract	代理母契約
60	foster mother（または rearing mother）	育ての母
61	prospective parent	これから親になる可能性がある人
62	custody	保護，監督，子供の養育権
63	exploitation	搾取
64	slippery slope theory	滑り坂理論
65	morning sickness	つわり
66	preterm birth	早産
67	full term birth	満期出産

15　終末期医療

	単語	意味
1	terminal care	終末期医療
2	palliative care	緩和ケア
3	vegetative state	植物状態
4	lethal dose	致死量
5	prolong	長引かせる，延長する
6	life-support system	生命維持装置
7	artificial respiration	人工呼吸
8	respirator	人工呼吸器
9	cardiopulmonary arrest	心肺停止
10	withhold	（治療を）差し控える
11	withdraw	引っ込める，（治療を）停止する
12	living will	リヴィング・ウィル
13	euthanasia	安楽死
14	physician-assisted suicide	医師による自殺幇助
15	mercy killing	慈悲殺，安楽死

16　臓器移植

	単語	意味
1	organ transplant	臓器移植
2	irreversible coma	不可逆的昏睡
3	acute rejection	急性拒絶反応
4	allocation	分配，割当
5	graft	移植，移植片
6	graft survival	移植臓器の生着率
7	xenograft transplantation	異種移植
8	xenotransplantation	異種移植
9	cadaveric donor	死体ドナー
10	deceased donor	死亡したドナー
11	cardiac arrest	心停止
12	living donor	生体ドナー
13	cardiologist	心臓専門医
14	cornea	角膜
15	immunosuppressive drug	免疫抑制剤
16	cyclosporine	シクロスポリン，サイクロスポリン：臓器移植者のための拒絶反応を抑える薬
17	diastolic blood pressure	最低血圧
18	systolic blood pressure	最大血圧
19	harvest	摘出（する）
20	recover	摘出する，回収する 注：harvest とほぼ同じ意味．現在では recover を使う方が好まれる．名詞形は recovery．
21	retrieve	recover, harvest と同じ意味．名詞形は retrieval．
22	organ donation	臓器提供
23	organ procurement	臓器の入手，臓器の獲得

| 24 | waiting list | 待機リスト |

17　ES 細胞・iPS 細胞

	単語	意味
1	blastocyst	胚盤胞
2	cleavage	卵割
3	differentiation	分化
4	embryo	胚
5	embryonic stem cell	ES 細胞
6	induced-pluripotent stem cell	人工多能性幹細胞，iPS 細胞
7	somatic (or adult) stem cells	体性幹細胞（体内のさまざまな組織に存在している幹細胞．骨髄にある造血幹細胞が典型例）
8	enucleation	除核
9	fetus	胎児
10	germ cell	生殖細胞
11	germ layer	胚葉
12	endoderm	内胚葉
13	mesoderm	中胚葉
14	ectoderm	外胚葉
15	unipotent stem cell	分化単能性の幹細胞：stem cells that have the ability to give rise to a single mature cell type of the body.
16	multipotent stem cell	多分化能のある幹細胞：stem cells that can give rise to a limited number of other cell types
17	pluripotent stem cell	多能性幹細胞：Stem cells that can develop into all the different cell types in the body except the placenta. They give rise to mulitpotent and unipotent stem cells as the embryo develops.
18	totipotent stem cells	全能性を有する幹細胞：the master cells of the body that contain all the genetic information needed to create all the cells of the body and the placenta.
19	parthenogenesis	単為生殖
20	paternal	父親の（⇔ maternal＝母親の）
21	regenerative medicine	再生医療［医学］
22	reprogram	初期化する
23	teratoma	奇形腫：未分化なヒト ES 細胞や iPS 細胞を治療等のために体内に移植した場合に，これらの細胞が異常な増殖を起こし，神経，軟骨，筋肉，粘膜などの多様な細胞からなる腫瘍を形成することがある．これを奇形種という．

18　老化

	単語	意味
1	aging	老化，高齢化
2	average life-span	平均寿命
3	longevity	長寿
4	senescence	老化
5	degenerative disease	変性疾患
6	dementia	認知症
7	mental retardation	精神遅滞
8	onset	発症

9	cognitive	認知の
10	recurrent	再発する
11	senile	老人性の
12	hibernation	冬眠
13	dormancy	冬眠状態
14	caloric restriction	カロリー制限

19　進化

	単語	意味
1	evolution	進化
2	evolutionary theory	進化論
3	natural selection	自然淘汰
4	eugenics	優生学
5	discrimination	差別
6	trait	形質
7	sterilize	断種する，不妊手術をする
8	anthropologist	人類学者

20　免疫・感染症

	単語	意味
1	communicable disease	伝染病
2	infectious disease	感染症
3	immunity	免疫
4	acquired immunity	獲得免疫，後天的免疫性
5	innate immunity	先天性免疫
6	herd immunity	集団免疫：集団内の多くの人がある感染症に対する予防接種を受けることで，集団全体の免疫力が上がり，その集団内でその感染症が流行する危険性が低くなる．この結果，集団内で予防接種を受けることが難しい層の人々（幼児や高齢者など）も，感染症から守られるようになること．
7	communicable disease (contagious disease, infectious disease)	伝染病，感染症
8	outbreak	発生
9	transmission	伝染
10	horizontal transmission	水平感染
11	vertical transmission	垂直感染
12	hospital-acquired infection	院内感染
13	nosocomial infection	院内感染
14	opportunistic infection	日和見感染
15	pathogen	病原体
16	infectious agent	病原菌
17	host cell	宿主細胞
18	microbe	微生物，細菌
19	bacteria	細菌
20	fungi	菌類
21	virus	ウイルス

22	retrovirus	レトロウイルス（遺伝情報として RNA をもつウイルス）
23	strain	種類，系統（type と捉えればよい）
24	toxin	毒素
25	antibiotic	抗生物質
26	drug-resistant bacteria	耐性菌
27	multiple-drug-resistant tuberculosis（MDR-TB）	多剤耐性結核
28	lymphatic system	リンパ系
29	tissue fluid	組織液
30	pus	膿
31	antigen	抗原
32	antibody	抗体
33	neutralize	中和する，無効化する
34	leukocyte	白血球
35	lymphocyte	リンパ球
36	acute hepatitis	急性肝炎
37	endemic	風土病，一地方特有の流行
38	epidemic	（広い地域で流行する）伝染病 ⇒ 例：中性のヨーロッパでの黒死病
39	pandemic	世界的大流行 ⇒ 例：1918 年のスペイン風邪
40	attenuated vaccine	弱毒化ワクチン
41	booster shot	（効能を促進するための）二度目の予防注射　cf. booster＝追加免疫
42	live vaccine	生ワクチン

〔参考〕endemic, epidemic, pandemic について
特定の集団や地域で比較的限定された期間内に通常期待される頻度を超えて同一疾患が多発することを epidemic という．流行はその規模により大流行（一国のほぼ全域にわたる場合）・汎流行（世界的な大流行の場合 =pandemic）・地方病的流行（局地的に地方病や風土病的疾患が長期間滞在的に流行している場合 =endemic）などと呼ばれる．
《南山堂，医学大辞典第 18 版より引用》

21　環境

	単語	意味
1	sustainable	維持できる，環境に優しい
2	deforestation	森林伐採
3	slash-and-burn	焼き畑式の
4	global warming	地球温暖化
5	carbon dioxide	二酸化炭素
6	fossil fuel	化石燃料
7	glacier	氷河
8	acid rain	酸性雨
9	latitude	緯度
10	longitude	経度
11	equator	赤道
12	habitat	生息地
13	photovoltaic power generation	太陽光発電
14	alternative energy	代替エネルギー
15	biodiversity	生物学的多様性
16	depletion	枯渇

17	deteriorate	悪化する
18	staple food	主食
19	fertilizer	肥料
20	erosion	浸食
21	extinction	絶滅
22	niche	隙間, 最適な場所, 生態的地位

22 動物・植物・その他

	単語	意味
1	avian	鳥 (の)
2	bovine	牛 (の)
3	canine	犬 (の)
4	feline	猫 (の)
5	simian	猿 (の)
6	swine	豚 (の)
7	primate	霊長類
8	humanoid	人造人間, ヒトに近い生物
9	rodent	げっ歯類
10	poultry	家禽類
11	vertebrate	脊椎動物
12	invertebrate	無脊椎動物
13	mammal	ほ乳類
14	reptile	は虫類
15	amphibian	両生類
16	microbe	微生物
17	herbivore	草食動物
18	carnivore	肉食動物
19	predator	捕食者
20	fungus	真菌類 (複数形が fungi)
21	pest	有害生物
22	pesticide	殺虫剤, 農薬
23	mold	カビ
24	flea	ノミ
25	tick	ダニ
26	pollen	花粉
27	stem	茎
28	trunk	幹
29	photosynthesis	光合成

23 化学・物理

	単語	意味
1	substance	物質
2	isotope	同位体
3	compound	化合物
4	organic compound	有機化合物

5	mineral	無機化合物，ミネラル
6	synthesis	合成
7	atom	原子
8	proton	陽子
9	electron	電子
10	neutron	中性子
11	molecule	分子
12	particle	粒子
13	property	特性
14	structure	構造
15	mass	質量
16	volume	体積
17	liquid	液体（＝fluid）
18	solid	固体
19	gas	気体
20	insoluble	不溶性の
21	dissolve	溶解する
22	solvent	溶媒
23	solute	溶質
24	solution	溶液
25	concentration	濃度
26	density	密度
27	component	構成要素，成分
28	ingredient	構成要素，成分
29	nutrient	栄養素
30	acid	酸
31	base	塩基
32	carbohydrate	炭水化物
33	protein	タンパク質
34	amino acid	アミノ酸
35	lipid	脂質
36	vitamin	ビタミン
37	nucleic acid	核酸
38	fat	脂肪
39	fatty acid	脂肪酸
40	enzyme	酵素
41	catalyst	触媒
42	starch	デンプン
43	chemical reaction	化学反応
44	bind to ～	～と結合する
45	specific	特異性のある，特定の
46	complementary	相補的な
47	sequence	配列
48	hydrogen bond	水素結合
49	fermentation	発酵

50	reagent	試薬
51	oxidation	酸化
52	reduction	還元
53	lactic acid	乳酸
54	sulfuric acid	硫酸
55	hydrochloric acid	塩酸
56	electric current	電流
57	evaporation	蒸発
58	gravity	重力
59	humidity	湿気，湿度
60	inertia	慣性
61	infrared ray	赤外線
62	ultraviolet ray	紫外線
63	momentum	運動量
64	static electricity	静電気
65	vapor	蒸気
66	velocity	速度

24　意外な意味をもつ英単語

	単語	意味
1	apply	（薬などを）塗る
2	control	対照群
3	culture	培養
4	harvest	（臓器を）摘出する
5	radical	根治の
6	sound	健全な，聴診する
7	theater	手術室
8	cardiac arrest	心停止
9	contract	病気にかかる，収縮する
10	release	弛緩する
11	focus	病巣
12	growth	腫瘍
13	fit	発作
14	regional	局所の（＝local）
15	vegetable	植物状態の患者
16	formula	処方箋
17	preparation	調合
18	rejection	拒絶反応
19	labor	陣痛
20	delivery	分娩
21	term	出産予定日
22	expecting	妊娠している
23	dispenser	薬剤師
24	intervention	医療行為
25	episode	症状の発現

26	consumption	肺結核
27	administer	投与する，（治療を）行う
28	compromise	傷つける，危うくする
29	admission	入院
30	discharge	退院
31	sustain	（被害などを）被る
32	alert	（患者などの）意識がはっきりしている
33	grade	病気の重さ，悪性度
34	canal	管
35	passage	継代培養
36	pupil	ひとみ，瞳孔
37	movement	便通（＝bowel movement）
38	eliminate	排泄する
39	be indicated	（治療や薬などが）必要である
40	medical procedure	医療処置
41	practice	開業，（医師の）業務
42	function	関数

25 増減の度合いを表す表現

増減表現はよく出てくるのでしっかりチェックしてほしい．

形容詞	副詞
steady（一定の，着実な）	steadily（着実に）
gradual（徐々の，漸進的な）	gradually（徐々に）
slight（わずかな）	slightly（わずかに）
sharp（急な）	sharply（急に）
rapid（急速な）	rapidly（急速に）
steep（急激な）	steeply（急激に）
sudden（突然の）	suddenly（突然に）
abrupt（突然の）	abruptly（突然に）
dramatic（劇的な）	dramatically（劇的に）
marked（著しい，顕著な）	markedly（著しく，顕著に）
remarkable（著しい）	remarkably（著しく）

例文1：There is a（または an）＿＿＿＿＿ increase in the number of people who get moderate exercise.
　　　　下線の箇所に上記の形容詞を状況に応じて入れていけばよい．

例文2：The number of people who get moderate exercise is increasing ＿＿＿＿＿ ．
　　　　下線の箇所に上記の副詞を状況に応じて入れていけばよい．

§2　学士試験合格のために覚えておきたい重要単語

　ここでは，過去に試験で出題された重要単語や，それに関連する単語を列挙した．大学入試レベルを超えている単語が多い．大学入試レベルの英単語の復習がある程度終わってから利用してもらったほうが効果的かもしれない．

1　動詞編

単語	意味
activate	活性化する
address	処理する，取り組む
administer	投与する
advocate	擁護する，支持する
afflict	苦しめる
aggregate	集まる，集める
alleviate	（苦痛などを）弱める，軽減する　同義語：attenuate, abate, lessen, mitigate, weaken
allocate	割り当てる　同義語：assign, allot
ameliorate	改善する，良くなる　同義語：improve
amplify	拡大する，増幅する
augment	増加させる
backfire	裏目に出る
be compounded	悪化する
blunt	鈍らせる，弱める（「鈍い」という意味の形容詞にもなる）
categorize	分類する　同義語：assort, classify, sort out
circumvent	避ける　同義語：avoid, evade, sidestep
choke	窒息させる　同義語：smother, suffocate
cleave	切り裂く　　cf. cleavage＝裂け目，卵割
coerce	強制する
coax	説得する，導く
comprise	構成する
compromise	害を与える（damage），弱める（weaken）
concur	同時に起こる
confer	与える
contaminate	汚染する
convince	納得させる，確信させる
corroborate	裏付ける，補強する　同義語：confirm
culminate in ～	結果的に～なる　同義語：result in ～
curb	抑制する　同義語：restrain, check, suppress
debilitate	衰弱させる　同義語：weaken, sap　cf. debilitating（形）＝衰弱させていく
decipher	解読する
degrade	分解する
deplete	使い果たす，枯渇させる
deploy	利用する，配置する
deposit	沈着させる，沈着（名詞にもなる）
deteriorate	悪化する
differentiate	分化する，区別する
diffuse	拡散する
dilute	薄める
discard	捨てる　同義語：dispose of ～
discharge	退院させる
discriminate	差別する，識別する
disinfect	消毒する，殺菌する　同義語：sterilize

disperse	普及させる，広める　同義語：disseminate
dissect	解剖する，詳しく調べる　同義語：anatomize
dissociate	分離する
distort	歪める
elicit	引き出す，導き出す
enhance	高める
entail	〜を伴う　同義語：involve
entangle	もつれさせる，巻き込む　cf. tangle＝もつれ
entice	気を引く，誘惑する
eradicate	根絶する
estimate	見積もる，推定する
evoke	誘発する，引き起こす　同義語：provoke
exacerbate	悪化させる　同義語：aggravate, worsen
excrete	排泄する
extrapolate	推定する，（拡張して）適用する，当てはめる
facilitate	促進する
fine-tune	微調整する　同義語：tweak
fluctuate	変動する
forge	作り上げる
forgo	〜なしで済ませる　同義語：do without 〜
fund	資金を提供する
glow	輝く，真っ赤に燃える
halt	止める，止まる（「停止」という意味の名詞にもなる）
halve	半減する　cf. double＝2倍になる，triple＝3倍になる，quadruple＝4倍になる
harness	利用する
impair	弱める，害を与える
implement	実行する
incorporate	組み込む
incubate	培養する，孵化する
inflict	（苦痛など）を与える
ingest	摂取する
inhibit	抑制する，妨げる　cf. inhibitor＝阻害剤
intensify	強める，激しくする
localize	局在させる　cf. local（形容詞）＝局所的な
modulate	調節する
offset	相殺する
optimize	最適化する
outlive	〜より長生きする
outcompete	〜に競争で勝つ，競争の末〜を駆逐する
outweigh	〜より重要である
negate	無効にする，否定する
pinpoint	正確に指摘する（記述する）
plummet	減少する　同義語：decline, decrease, diminish, shrink
plunge	突っ込む，急落する
postulate	仮定する
prevent	妨げる　同義語：bar, hamper, hinder, impede, obstruct, preclude, thwart

probe	調べる，探り針
procreate	子をもうける，子を産む
prohibit	禁止する　同義語：ban, forbid
proliferate	増殖する　同義語：multiply
propagate	増殖させる，繁殖させる，増殖する
purify	精製する
relinquish	捨てる，断念する
remove	除去する　同義語：eliminate, get rid of 〜
resuscitate	蘇生させる
scrutinize	精査する
segregate	分離する，隔離する　同義語：isolate, quarantine
sequence	配列を決定する（「配列」という名詞にもなる）
serve	役立つ，役割を果たす，機能する
sift	ふるいにかける
skew	歪める，歪曲する
skyrocket	急上昇する
spark	引き起こす　同義語：bring about 〜, give rise to 〜, lead to 〜, result in 〜, cause, engender, induce, mediate, trigger
spawn	産む，引き起こす
spoil	駄目にする　同義語：flaw, ruin
stratify	階層に分ける
strive to do 〜	〜しようと努力する
subvert	倒す，破壊する
supervise	監督する，監視する　同義語：oversee
surge	（急に）増える　同義語：increase, soar, swell
truncate	切断する，切り取る　同義語：amputate（特に外科手術の場合）
underlie	〜の基礎となる
undermine	破壊する　同義語：destroy, disrupt
underscore	強調する　同義語：emphasize, highlight, stress, underline
uphold	支持する　同義語：endorse, support
validate	〜が正しいことを証明する（＝confirm the validity of 〜）　同義語：verify
wane	衰える，弱くなる
wean	離乳させる，引き離す
withhold	与えないでおく，差し控える

2　名詞編

単語	意味
ablation	切除
advent	到来，出現
aftermath	余波，結果，後遺症
agenda	検討課題，協議事項
ailment	病気，疾患　同義語：illness, disease, disorder, infirmity, malady
aim	目的　同義語：end, goal, object, objective, purpose
altruism	利他主義　cf. altruistic＝利他的な
anomaly	異常，不合理
assay	試験，分析

autopsy	検死，死体解剖
biopsy	生体組織検査
breeding ground	温床
bruise	打撲
breakthrough	大成功，大躍進
building block	基礎的要素，構成要素
by-product	副産物
cessation	停止　同義語：arrest, halt
cluster	集団，一群
coincidence	同時発生，一致
complications	合併症
component	構成要素，成分　同義語：constituent, ingredient
concern	懸念，関心事
conundrum	難問　同義語：puzzle, riddle
constraint	制限，制約
convulsion	痙攣（けいれん）　同義語：spasm
countermeasure	対策，対抗手段
coverage	保険がきく範囲，保険が適用される範囲
culprit	犯人，原因
deficit	不足　同義語：dearth, deficiency, insufficiency, lack, paucity, scarcity, shortage
diagnosis	診断
dichotomy	二分法
discrepancy	不一致，食い違い
disparity	不均衡
dose	服用量，放射線量
duration	持続，持続期間
efficacy	効能，効果
epicenter	震央，発生地，中心点
expertise	専門的知識
fallacy	誤った考え
flaw	欠陥，欠点　同義語：defect, downside, drawback, fault, shortcoming
fluorescence	蛍光，蛍光性
fracture	骨折
fragment	断片　同義語：segment
gestation	妊娠　同義語：conception, pregnancy
hype	誇大広告，麻薬常用者，皮下注射（器）
immunity	免疫
immunization	予防接種　同義語：vaccination
implications（主に複数形で）	影響　同義語：effect, influence, ramification, repercussion
incidence	発生率
initiative	新しい戦略，率先した取り組み
incision	切開　　cf. 動詞形は incise
intake	摂取
integrity	完全性（欠陥や傷がない状態），誠実
interplay	相互作用　同義語：interaction

intervention	医療行為，医療措置　同義語：medical procedure
landmark	画期的な出来事　同義語：milestone
lapse	誤り，失敗　同義語：blunder, error, mistake
last resort	最後の手段
lesion	病変，損傷
makeover	大変身，改革
malfunction	機能不全
malnutrition	栄養失調
malpractice	医療過誤
manifestation	症状，徴候　同義語：symptom
maneuver	（技術を要する）操作，戦略
morbidity	疾病率，病的状態
mortality	死亡率
neonate	新生児
nutrient	栄養素
nutrition	栄養　同義語：nourishment
onset	発症　同義語：development
onus	義務，責任
outbreak	発生
outreach	奉仕活動
paw	足，手（イヌやネコなどの）
pediatrician	小児科医
plagiarism	盗作，盗用
plight	困難，苦境　同義語：difficulty, predicament, quandary
platform	基盤
precaution	警戒，予防策
precursor	先駆者，前駆体
preservative	保存料
prevalence	有病率，普及率
probability	見込み（または可能性）　同義語：likelihood, odds, possibility, prospect
progeny	子孫　同義語：descendant, offspring, posterity
propensity	傾向　同義語：tendency
prophylaxis	予防
puberty	思春期　同義語：adolescence
radiation	放射線，放射能
range	範囲　同義語：extent, scope, spectrum
regimen	投薬計画，処方計画
rejection	拒絶，拒絶反応
resurgence	再発　同義語：recurrence, relapse
rupture	破裂
scaffold	足場
scar	傷跡
scrub	ごしごし洗う
seizure	発作　同義語：attack, fit
sewage	下水
side effect	副作用　同義語：adverse event

stimulus	刺激　同義語：incentive
stitch	ひと針，ひと縫い（動詞では「縫合する」）
stratum	層，階層
stride	進歩
subsidy	補助金　同義語：grant
supervision	監督，監視　同義語：oversight, surveillance
tactic	戦略
threshold	閾値
trade-off	相殺取引，交換
trajectory	軌道，経路
tremble	震え　同義語：tremor
twist	ねじれ，曲解，歪曲，意外な展開 cf. 動詞では「ねじる」「捻挫する」「歪曲する」という意味
underpinning	土台，基盤
uptake	取り込み，吸い上げ
variable	変数，変わりやすい（形容詞）
ward	病棟，区

3　形容詞編

単語	意味
aberrant	異常な　同義語：abnormal, anomalous, unusual
accountable	説明する責任がある
adjuvant	補助の，補助的薬剤（名詞にもなる）
adverse	有害な 同義語：deleterious, detrimental, harmful, injurious　　cf. toxic＝有毒な
aggressive	積極的な，攻撃的な，侵略的な
anecdotal	非科学的な，科学的客観性がない　同義語：unscientific cf. anecdote＝逸話，個人的な経験に基づく話（科学的な根拠がない話）
anterior	前方の　　反意語：posterior＝後ろの
causal	原因となる，因果関係を示す　cf. causal relationship＝因果関係
comparable	匹敵する，比較できる
compatible	両立しうる，適合性がある
competent	判断能力がある
concomitant	同時に生じる，付随する
confidential	秘密の　　cf. confidentiality＝守秘義務
considerable	かなりの　同義語：substantial
controversial	議論を呼ぶような，問題のある，意見が分かれる 同義語：contentious, disputable, at issue
conventional	従来の，伝統的な，型にはまった
critical	重要な　同義語：crucial, important, relevant, pivotal, vital
cumulative	累積的な
cutting-edge	最先端の　同義語：state-of-the-art
daunting	非常に困難な，人の気力をくじくような
deficient	不足している　同義語：insufficient, lacking, scant
devastating	破壊的な，衝撃的な，圧倒的な
disproportionate	不均衡な，釣り合いが取れていない
dormant	冬眠中の，睡眠状態の

eligible	資格のある，ふさわしい
elusive	理解しづらい，捉えどころがない，達成困難な
empirical	経験による
equivocal	あいまいな 同義語：ambiguous, obscure, vague　反意語：unequivocal＝明白な
essential	必要不可欠な　同義語：indispensable, vital
feasible	実行可能な　同義語：viable
full-blown	満開の，病状が進んだ
fundamental	基本的な　同義語：basic, rudimentary, underlying
futile	無駄な，無益な
identical	同一の
impartial	公平な，偏りがない
implicit	暗黙の　反意語：explicit＝明確な
incoherent	一貫していない　同義語：inconsistent
incurable	不治の
indiscriminate	無差別の
inevitable	必然的な，避けられない
intensive	集中的な　　cf. intensive care＝集中治療
intractable	治療しづらい，扱いにくい
intravenous	静脈内の，静脈注射の（名詞では「静脈注射」という意味）
intricate	複雑な　同義語：complex, complicated
intriguing	大変興味深い（＝very interesting）
invasive	侵襲的な
inverse	逆の，反比例の
irreversible	不可逆的な
lateral	横の，側面の
lethal	致命的な　同義語：deadly, fatal
longitudinal	縦の，経度の，長期的な　cf. longitude＝経度
massive	大きくて重い
municipal	都市の，地方自治体の
myriad	無数の
optical	視覚の，光学の
optimal	最適の，最善の
overt	明らかな　反意語：covert＝隠された
quantitative	定量的な（「数値で表せる」というイメージが重要） 反意語：qualitative＝定性的な
plausible	妥当な，正しそうに見える
populous	人口が多い
reciprocal	相互の　同義語：mutual
robust	強固な（＝strong）
skeptical	疑い深い　cf. skepticism＝疑い
senile	老人の，老年の　cf. senile dementia＝老年性認知症
stringent	厳格な　同義語：rigid, rigorous, stern, strict
spatial	空間の（space の形容詞形）
startling	驚くべき，衝撃的な　同義語：surprising, astonishing, stunning
sufficient	十分な　同義語：enough, adequate

単語	意味
sweeping	全面的な，徹底的な，一掃するような
tangible	明白な　同義語：clear, evident, obvious　cf. intangible＝つかみどころがない
transient	一時的な
tantalizing	興味をかき立てるような
unprecedented	先例のない
urgent	差し迫った　同義語：imminent, impending, pressing
versatile	多才な，用途が広い
virulent	毒性の強い
vulnerable	傷つきやすい，弱い

4 副詞編

単語	意味
accordingly	したがって，それゆえ　同義語：hence, therefore
alternatively	その代わりに
apparently	明らかに　同義語：evidently, clearly, obviously
collectively	まとめると　同義語：in conclusion, in summary,
considerably	かなり　同義語：substantially
constitutively	恒常的に
conversely	逆に
dramatically	劇的に
exclusively	独占的に，もっぱら
extensively	広範囲にわたって，広く，大規模に
furthermore	さらに，その上　同義語：additionally, in addition, moreover
meanwhile	その一方で，その間に
overwhelmingly	圧倒的に
presumably	おそらく，たぶん
readily	容易に，すぐに
relatively	比較的，相対的に
remarkably	著しく，意外なことに（文頭で）　同義語：strikingly, markedly,
specifically	特に，具体的に言えば
subsequently	その次に，後で
thereby	それによって
undoubtedly	間違いなく，明らかに
virtually	事実上，ほぼ

5 熟語編

単語	意味
abstain from ～	（お酒など）を慎む，控える　cf. abstention＝節制
act on ～	～に作用する，～に従って行動する
across the board	全体的に，全面的に，
add up to ～	合計で～になる，結局～ということになる　同義語：amount to ～
apart from ～	～を除いて
ascribe A to B	AをBのせいにする　同義語：attribute A to B
as compared with ～	～と比較して
at length	徹底的に，長い間，ついに
at stake	危険にさらされている，問題となっている

at the mercy of ～	～のなすがままである
at the same time	同時に、しかしながら
be affiliated with ～	～に所属している、～と提携している
be associated with ～	～と関連がある　cf.「～と結合している」という意味になることもある．同義語：be related to ～
be at odds with ～	～と争っている、～と意見が食い違っている
be attributable to ～	～に起因する
be involved in ～	～に関与する　同義語：be implicated in ～
be on the verge of ～	今にも～しようとしている、～する寸前である 同義語：be on the point of ～, be on the edge of ～
be riddled with ～	～でいっぱいである、～だらけである
be rooted in ～	～に基づいている　同義語：be based on ～
be projected to do ～	～すると予測されている
be purported to do ～	～だと考えられている、噂では～だとされている
be susceptible to ～	～にかかりやすい　同義語：be liable to ～, be predisposed to ～
by a factor of ～（「～」には数が入る）	～倍に、～倍だけ 例：The risk increased by a factor of 3.（危険性が3倍だけ増えた）
call on 人 to do ～	人に～するように要求する
come to light	明るみに出る
count on ～	～を当てにする、～を頼りにする　同義語：depend on ～, rely on ～
figure out ～	～を理解する
fly in the face of ～	～に公然と反対する
focus on ～	～に焦点を当てる　同義語：zero in on ～, home in on ～
go far	大いに役立つ　同義語：go a long way
go to any lengths to do ～	～するためにどんなことでもする
have O in common (with ～)	(～と) O を共有している
have difficulty doing ～	～するのに苦労する 同義語：have trouble doing ～, have a hard time doing ～
have important implications for ～	～に重要な影響を与える
have nothing to do with ～	～と何の関係もない
gain ground	成功する、支持を得る、受け入れられる
in an effort to do ～	～にするために（目的を表す） 同義語：in an attempt to do ～, in a bid to do ～
in contrast	対照的に　同義語：by contrast
in light of ～	～を考慮に入れると
in response	それに応じて（前の文の内容を受けて文頭で使われることが多い）
in particular	特に
in place	適当な位置に、環境が整って cf. working（正常に機能している）, ready to work（準備が整っている） cf. put O in place＝O を実施する、O を整備する
in summary	要約すると　同義語：in short, in sum
in terms of ～	～との関連で、～の点から
in the fourth decade of life	30歳代で（「40歳代」ではないことに注意）
in the face of ～	～に直面して、～にもかかわらず
in the wake of ～	～の後に
keep O at bay（O には病気などが入る）	O を寄せ付けない、O を食い止めておく

keep O in check	O を抑制する
level off	横ばいになる
make up for ～	～の埋め合わせをする
on call	呼び出しにいつでも応じられる，（医者などが）待機している
opt out	義務を逃れる（臓器移植の英文では，「本人が生前に臓器提供をしないという意思表示をする」という意味になる）
prior to ～	～より前に
prompt 人 to do ～	人に～するように促す　同義語：urge 人 to do ～, drive 人 to do ～
provide (an) insight into ～	～を理解するための手がかりをもたらす
refer to A as B	A を B と呼ぶ
regardless of ～	～に関係なく
replace A with B	A の代わりに B を用いる，A を B と取り替える
rule out ～	～を除外する
set O in motion	O を作動させる，O を引き起こす
shed light on ～	～を明らかにする，～を解明する　同義語：clarify, elucidate
sign up for ～	～に参加することを約束する
S is characterized by ～	「S の特徴は～である」と意訳してよい．直訳は「S は～によって特徴づけられる」．
spill over	波及する，飛び火する
stem from ～	～から生じる，～に由来する　同義語：derive from ～
stick to ～	～に固執する　同義語：adhere to ～, cling to ～
stumble on ～	～を偶然発見する
succumb to ～	～に屈する，～で死ぬ
take its toll on ～	～に被害（損失・犠牲）をもたらす，～に有害な影響を与える
take O into account	O を考慮に入れる
think outside the box	独創的な考え方をする，型にはまらない考え方をする
think twice about ～	～について考え直す，～をためらう　同義語：have second thought(s) about ～
to date	今までのところ　同義語：so far
with respect to ～	～に関して　同義語：with regard to ～
work on ～	～に取り組む

§3　知っておくと参考になる接頭辞と接尾辞

接頭辞	意味	例
acro-	先端，高所	acrophobia＝高所恐怖症　　acronym＝頭字語
angio-	血管	angiogenesis＝血管新生
ante-	前の	anterior＝前の
arterio-	動脈	arteriosclerosis＝動脈硬化
astro-	星	astrocyte＝アストロサイト（グリア細胞の1つ．グリア細胞とは，ニューロンを囲んでその役割をサポートする役目を果たしている細胞） cf.　astronomy＝天文学
audio-	聴，音	auditory＝聴覚の
bi-	2つ	bipolar＝両極の　　bilateral＝双方の，両側の
bio-	生命，生物	biodiversity＝生物多様性　　bioluminescence＝生物発光
cardio-	心臓	cardiovascular＝心臓血管の
dermato-	皮膚	dermatitis＝皮膚炎
dys-	不良，障害	dysfunction＝機能障害　　dyslexia＝難読症
endo-	内部	endoscope＝内視鏡　　endogenous＝内因性の

epi-	間に，上に，	epidemic＝伝染病（の流行）→ dem は「人々」という意味．よって，この単語には「人々の間に」という意味が読み取れる． epidermis＝表皮　　epicenter＝震央
eu-	良い	eugenics＝優生学　　euthanasia＝安楽死（thana は「死」という意味 cf. thanatology＝死生学）
gastro-	胃	gastrointestinal＝胃腸の　　gastrin＝ガストリン（胃から出るホルモン）
hemi-	半分	hemisphere＝半球
hemo-	血液	hemophilia＝血友病　　hemorrhage＝大出血
hetero-	異なった	heterogeneous＝異種の，異質の
homeo-	類似の	homeostasis＝恒常性　　homeopathy＝同毒療法
homo-	同一の	homogeneous＝同質の
hypo-	下に	hypodermic＝皮下の hypothesis＝仮説（仮説とは，何かを説明する際の下敷きになる考え）
macro-	大きい	macromolecule＝巨大分子
mal-	悪い	malnutrition＝栄養失調　　malpractice＝医療過誤
mega-	巨大	megaphone＝拡声器
meta-	変化，超える	metabolism＝代謝　　metastasis＝転移，変性
micro-	微小	microbe＝微生物　　microstructure＝微細構造
multi-	多数の	multicellular organism＝多細胞生物
neuro-	神経	neurology＝神経学
omni-	すべて	omnipotent＝全能なる神，全能の
pan-	すべてに渡る	pandemic＝世界的大流行　　panacea＝万能薬
peri-	周りの，近い	perinatal＝周産期の　　peripheral＝周辺部にある，周囲の perimenopausal＝閉経期前後の
physio-	身体	physiology＝生理学　　physiotherapy＝理学療法
post-	後に	postnatal＝産後の　　postoperative＝術後の
psycho-	精神	psychology＝心理学　　psychoanalysis＝精神分析
radio-	放射線，放射能	radiation＝放射線　　radioactive＝放射能をもった　　radiologist＝放射線科医

接尾辞	意味	例
-borne	〜によって運ばれる	airborne infection＝空気感染　　foodborne illness＝食中毒 mosquito-borne＝蚊によって媒介される
-cide	殺す	pesticide＝殺虫剤　　herbicide＝除草剤
-gamy	結婚	monogamy＝一夫一婦制　　polygamy＝一夫多妻制
-gen	生じさせるもの	carcinogen＝発癌物質　　pathogen＝病原体
-itis	炎症	arthritis＝関節炎　　bronchitis＝気管支炎　　hepatitis＝肝炎
-meter	計測器	thermometer＝温度計
-oid	似る	android＝人造人間　　opioid＝オピオイド（鎮痛薬の１つ．「アヘン（opium）に似ている（oid）」という成り立ちになっている）
-osis	症	osteoporosis＝骨粗鬆症　　pollinosis＝花粉症
-phobia	恐怖症	xenophobia＝外人恐怖症
-scope	〜を見る器械，〜鏡	microscope＝顕微鏡　　endoscope＝内視鏡　　stethoscope＝聴診器
-tomy	切断，切除	anatomy＝解剖，解剖学　　mastectomy＝乳房切除術　　osteotomy＝骨切り術

索　引

〔欧文索引〕

abortion　27
allele　47, 57
ALS　42
Alzheimer's disease　55
blood test　55
BSE　144
cancer　5
childbed fever　18
chromosome　47
cloning　27
compliance　31
coronary heart disease　52
CT　3, 5, 77
dementia　55
diabete　49, 52
DNA　15
DNA analysis　56
Down syndrome　56
euthanasia　27
gene therapy　27
genetic testing　27
genome　37
HIV　62
homeostasis　1
human genome project　37
infant mortality　53
infection　18
influenza　62
informed consent　34
medical education　23
medical ethics　23
medical practice　31
medical student　22
memory　10
microbe　13
mutant　47
neuron　10
obesity　1, 49
organ transplant　27
pandemic　62
phenotype　53

phenylketonuria　39
physician-assisted suicide　27
pneumonia　55
SARS　62
stem cell　42
thrifty gene　134
X-ray　3, 5, 55

〔和文索引〕

iPS細胞　124
アドレナリン　134
アルツハイマー病　137
ES細胞　124
遺伝子検査　17, 83
遺伝子再集合　143
遺伝子診断　93
遺伝子治療　93
遺伝性疾患　128
インスリン　131
インフォームドコンセント　117
インフルエンザ　143
エイズ　144
オーダーメイド医療　120
科学　28
鎌状赤血球貧血症　128
癌　129
感染症　143
狂犬病　144
虚血性心疾患　129
クラインフェルター症候群　128
クローン技術　124
結核　144
血友病　128
下痢　99
顕微鏡　82
抗ガン剤　122
高脂血症　129
抗生物質　100, 143
コレステロール　140
再興感染症　144

自殺幇助　100
実験動物　100
ジフテリア　144
出生前診断　83
新興感染症　144
新生児スクリーニング　83
染色体異常症　128
1000ドルゲノムプロジェクト　120
多因子遺伝病　128
ダウン症　128
単一遺伝子疾患　128
着床前診断　83
デュシェンヌ型筋ジストロフィー　128
糖尿病　129, 131
ドリー　127
鳥インフルエンザ　144
ニューロン　79
妊娠　136
認知症　137
脳死　100
囊胞性線維症　128
肺炎　99
肺ガン　122
発癌リスク　4, 74
ハンチントン病　128
パンデミック　143
微生物　81
ヒトゲノム　120
肥満　70, 134
HeLa細胞　115
フェニルケトン尿症　83, 122
ヘルシンキ宣言　116
放射線　4, 73
マラリア　99, 144
慢性骨髄性白血病　128
ミトコンドリア遺伝病　129
メタゲノミクス　82
網膜芽細胞腫　128
ワクチン　143

著者紹介

土田 治（つちだ おさむ）
　2000年 東京大学大学院法学政治学研究科 修士課程修了
　現　在 河合塾KALS英語講師

NDC460　191p　26 cm

医学部編入への英語演習（いがくぶへんにゅうへのえいごえんしゅう）

2013年3月27日　第1刷発行
2016年7月15日　第4刷発行

監　修　河合塾KALS（かわいじゅく カルス）
著　者　土田　治（つちだ おさむ）
発行者　鈴木　哲
発行所　株式会社　講談社
　　　　〒112–8001　東京都文京区音羽2-12-21
　　　　　販売　(03) 5395–4415
　　　　　業務　(03) 5395–3615
編　集　株式会社　講談社サイエンティフィク
　　　　代表　矢吹俊吉
　　　　〒162–0825　東京都新宿区神楽坂2-14　ノービィビル
　　　　　編集　(03) 3235–3701
DTP　　株式会社エヌ・オフィス
印刷所　株式会社平河工業社
製本所　株式会社国宝社

　落丁本・乱丁本は購入書店名を明記のうえ，講談社業務宛にお送り下さい．送料小社負担にてお取替えします．なお，この本の内容についてのお問い合わせは，講談社サイエンティフィク宛にお願いいたします．定価はカバーに表示してあります．

© Osamu Tsuchida, 2013

本書のコピー，スキャン，デジタル化等の無断複製は著作権法上での例外を除き禁じられています．本書を代行業者等の第三者に依頼してスキャンやデジタル化することはたとえ個人や家庭内の利用でも著作権法違反です．

JCOPY　〈(社) 出版者著作権管理機構　委託出版物〉

複写される場合は，その都度事前に (社) 出版者著作権管理機構（電話 03-3513-6969, FAX 03-3513-6979, e-mail: info@jcopy.or.jp）の許諾を得てください．

Printed in Japan

ISBN978-4-06-153886-3